Philosophy

Philosophy

A Short, Visual Introduction

Minneapolis
Fortress Press

PHILOSOPHY

A Short, Visual Introduction

Christianity and the Liberal Arts

Cover and book design: Joseph Novak

Library of Congress Cataloging-in-Publication Data is available

Paperback ISBN: 978-1-4514-9237-8

eBook ISBN: 978-1-5064-0148-5

The paper used in this publication meets the minimum requirements of American National Standard for Information Sciences — Permanence of Paper for Printed Library Materials, ANSI Z329.48-1984.

Manufactured in the U.S.A.

table of contents

SERIES INTRODUCTION

SCOTT PAETH
GENERAL EDITOR

Once, to be an educated person in Western culture meant to be educated in the liberal arts. The classical educational system of European society, passed down from the medieval university system to the modern age, emphasized a broadly based grounding in the humanities. Knowledge of history, literature, philosophy, and art were all seen as being the essential building blocks, not simply of a university degree, but of a well-lived life. Over the past several decades that presupposition has eroded significantly as Western education has undergone significant changes. It is no longer assumed that Christians in the United States in the early part of the twenty-first century have the kind of background knowledge that was once taken for granted in the study of theology, bible, or church history. What's more, Christian life in the twenty-first century requires an expanded base of knowledge beyond what was once deemed adequate. In particular, in a global society, students increasingly need to know about cultures and religions outside of European Christianity.

Christianity and the Liberal Arts is intended to address this need. By offering a series of easy to read and accessible introductions to subjects that are crucial to theological formation, we hope to give students resources that will help them to understand the often complex questions that arise in the context of theological study. These volumes assume no prior knowledge of their subject matter, but offer the essential ideas, events, and figures that comprise the disciplines of the humanities. Our hope in providing these resources is that they will be used as guides into a deeper exploration of the liberal arts, so that they may be not only well prepared for theological study but also humanely educated participants in the Christian life.

VOLUME INTRODUCTION

SCOTT PAETH

Until recently, it could be taken for granted that college graduates would be well acquainted with the major thinkers and traditions of the Western philosophical tradition. Even students who had not majored in philosophy could at least be expected to understand the basic contours of Plato's metaphysics, Aristotle's ethics, or Hegel's dialectic. Teachers of theology and religion could assume this background. However, changes in higher education over the last half century have rendered that assumption problematic. Students often graduate with little or no prior experience with philosophy and, as a result, many of the complex questions regarding the relationship of philosophy and theology and the philosophical language that undergirds much of theological discourse become much more difficult to address.

At the same time, access to information about all subjects, philosophy included, has become more and more widely accessible to anyone with an interest. Online resources offer myriad opportunities for a "quick and dirty" perspective on any discipline, movement, or idea that one could desire. However, despite improvements in many online resources in recent years, they continue to suffer from issues of "quality control," which can create misinformation and misunderstanding. Many Christian laypeople who turn to such resources without proper guidance wanting to know more about the history of their faith and its philosophical underpinnings may find them less than helpful.

This volume is intended for such learners, both in the classroom and in the pew. It provides a broad overview of the main trends of Western philosophical thought and some of the major figures from the ancient period to the postmodern era. While not intended to be a comprehensive or detailed introduction to the history of philosophy, it is intended to provide the main ideas and overall trajectory of its development over the last 2,500 years. Our hope is that the format of this volume will enable readers to grasp the key concepts of a number of the most influential figures in philosophy and begin to see their relevance to the study of theology.

Given the limitations of space, a number of figures and movements that would have been appropriate for a volume such as this were excluded. Our goal was to focus particularly on those figures who were most influential to the development of theology as it is studied today. Among the challenges that such an approach presents is in providing a balance, not only in terms of historical period and philosophical school, but also in terms of issues of ethnicity and gender representation. We wish we could say that the history of Western philosophy offered ample opportunities to include the voices of women and non-Europeans. Unfortunately, this is not the case, and there is a great deal of critique that can be offered of the entirety of Western philosophy on those grounds. However, when possible we did strive to include voices that did not conform to the white, male, heteronormative default. For the most part, these are found in the sections on twentieth-century and contemporary philosophy, because it has only recently been the case that these voices have been permitted into the fold of mainstream philosophical discourse. Where it was possible to do so, we have sought to highlight those voices.

This volume is a concentrated dose of philosophy, designed to get you started on your own journey of philosophical inquiry and growth. It is not a substitute for going directly to the sources and reading them for yourself, but we hope it will serve as an introduction and a guide, in order to enable you to enter into the philosophical stream without being swept away. Philosophy is an endlessly fascinating subject, which has implications for every dimension of life and faith, and which is in continual dialogue with the Christian theological tradition. Without an adequate grasp of philosophy, it is not possible to develop an adequate grasp of theology. If, in the end, this book excites your intellect and imagination and drives you to explore these issues further, then we will count that as a success. What's more, if this volume aids you in grappling with the philosophical issues that are intertwined with the study of theology, we will count that as a success as well.

ONE

AN
CIE
NT

The safes
al charact
ation of th
an philos
dition is th
ts of a seri
notes to

—t gener-
—eriz-
—e Europe-
—ophical tra-
—at it consis-
—es of foot-
Plato.[1]

[1] ALFRED NORTH WHITEHEAD, *PROCESS AND REALITY*, 39

PLATO

Alfred North Whitehead once remarked that all of philosophy is a series of footnotes to Plato. Whether or not that is actually the case, Plato has certainly wielded an enormous influence on every philosopher who came after him, and by extension, has been an enormously influential figure in theology. Platonic philosophy undergirds the work of many of the great early Christian theologians, such as Origen and Augustine, as well as the mystical theology of Pseudo-Dionysius and his influence continues to be felt in Christian theology.

There were philosophers prior to Plato's time, but, as with so many other things, they are defined in relationship to the work of Plato and Socrates, and thus are usually referred to as "pre-Socratic" philosophers. Very little remains of their work, and what does remain exists only in fragments. They were a diverse group.

Thales of Miletus believed that all things derived from water, while Anaximenes believed they derived from air. Anaximander argued that they derived from a separate, unnamed substance. Meanwhile, Pythagoras attempted to understand all of reality in terms of numbers.

Heraclitus, one of the best known of the pre-Socratics, believed that all things were in flux, and nothing was constant, while Parmenides argued that the appearance of motion was an illusion, and all things were simply manifestations of an unchanging being. His pupil Zeno was known for formulating paradoxical riddles to illustrate this idea, such as proving that motion was impossible by demonstrating that movement of any distance required one to first travel half of that distance, which first required moving half of *that* distance, and so on. What unified the pre-Socratic philosophers was not a particular philosophical perspective, but their interest in discovering what it was that defined the *essence* of reality.

Plato, who lived in the fifth century BCE, was a student of the first great Athenian philosopher, Socrates. Socrates was known for walking the streets of Athens stopping passersby and quizzing them about what they claimed to know. In doing so, he attempted to demonstrate that they did not actually possess genuine knowledge, but only poorly grounded opinions about the nature of the world. Socrates himself never claimed to know anything, and according to the Oracle at Delphi, this actually made him the wisest of all. Socrates viewed himself not so much as a teacher but as a gadfly, pestering his fellow Athenians in order to reveal to them their ignorance. This was, as one can imagine, annoying. Nevertheless, he developed a following among the young men of Athens, who saw him as challenging the social, political, and religious presuppositions of a society that they were themselves questioning.

To them, I said, the truth would be literally nothing but the shadows of the image

Their souls are ever hastening into the upper world where they desire to dwell.

Plato, *De Republica*, Book VII

At the time, there was another group of public thinkers who were active in Athens, known as the "sophists." Unlike Socrates, the sophists advertised themselves as possessing actual knowledge that they were happy to share—for a price. The sophists were often portrayed as engaging in pointless argumentation for its own sake, rather than teaching any genuine knowledge (thus giving birth to the term "sophistry" to describe deceptive argumentation). The playwright Aristophanes made fun of them in his comedy *The Clouds*, lumping Socrates in their fold, despite his insistence on his own ignorance and his refusal, unlike the sophists, to charge money. When *The Clouds* was performed, Socrates was apparently in the audience, and when the actor portraying him entered, he stood to allow the audience to see the resemblance between them.

Eventually Socrates was arrested and tried in Athens on charges of "corrupting the youth" of the city and making impious statements about the gods. His trial is recounted in Plato's dialogue the *Apology*, which consists largely of Socrates's defense against the charges. In spite of (or perhaps because of) his defense, Socrates was sentenced to death by a jury of Athenian citizens. Although he was given a chance to escape, Socrates accepted his sentence and died after drinking a cup of hemlock.

Building on Socrates's philosophy, Plato began to teach and write, founding the first university in Athens, known as the Academy. His writing primarily took the form of dialogues on moral and metaphysical questions between Socrates and an opponent or opponents. Most dialogues had a similar structure, in which Socrates would begin by posing a question, such as "What is justice?" or "What is piety?" to his conversation partner, who would then offer a definition. Socrates would then chip away at that definition until his adversary was forced to admit that they did not in fact know what they were talking about. The dialogues usually ended with both Socrates and his foe going their separate ways agreeing to continue thinking about the question.

Plato used this structure (and the character of Socrates) to pose philosophical problems for his students. Unlike Socrates, however, he did have some answers to offer. In his best known dialogue, *The Republic*, Plato presents a compelling picture of the relationship between knowledge, morality, politics, and the nature of reality itself.

The putative question in *The Republic* is "What is justice?" Socrates begins by knocking down a number of proposed answers to the question, before suggesting that justice is about the balance between three aspects of human nature: the mind, the heart, and the appetites. The just person is one whose mind and heart are allied with one another to keep their appetites under control, while those who are governed by their appetites are consumed by vice and live unjust lives. This leads Socrates and his conversation partners into a larger conversation about the nature of justice in society and what would be required to make a society that was not susceptible to the kind of corruption that they were familiar with from the recent history of Athens.

Eventually their conversation turns to questions of truth and knowledge, and here Plato offers one of his most enduring contributions to philosophy in the form of his Analogy of the Cave. Socrates asks his conversation partners to imagine a group of prisoners trapped together in a cave, forced to face a blank wall. Behind them, a light projects the shadows of various objects on the wall as they are carried past. What would happen, he asks, if one of those prisoners were freed and forced to turn around and face that light? He would see that the objects he had assumed to be real were merely images projected on a screen. If he were then taken up out of the cave, he would see the real objects rather than just their copies. First, he would look at their shadows on the ground, then at the objects themselves, until finally he could look up at the sun itself, as the source of illumination for these objects. He would

ideal

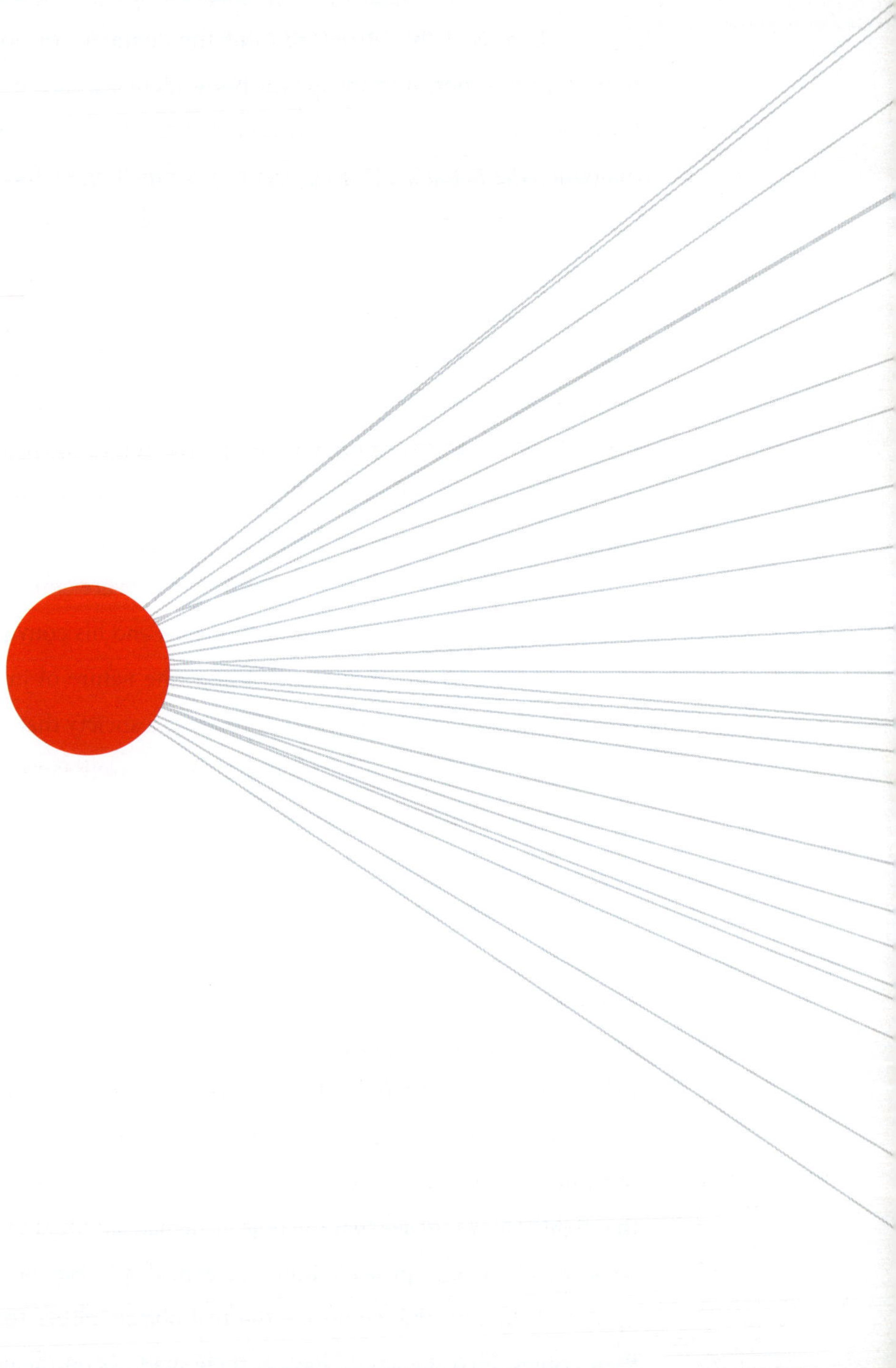

forms

have come to see the reality behind the images he had once taken to be real. Socrates then suggests that, if he were to go back to the cave and tell his fellow prisoners what he had seen, they would not believe him and would even kill him if it meant they could continue to live in their illusions.

The condition of the prisoners is akin to those who live their lives distracted by illusions, such as, in Plato's time, things like poetry and plays (television and video games would be apt contemporary analogues). The condition of those who are freed and come to know the objects that are projected behind them on the wall is akin to how we interact with the physical world around us. We perceive the world with our senses, but we lack knowledge of the reality that underlies those senses. This is why, when quizzed by Socrates, most of his opponents could not offer coherent answers. They could recognize justice or piety when they saw them, or identify physical objects such as horses or trees, but they could not explain *why* those things were what they were. In order for that to take place, they needed to go beyond the world of sense perception.

This leads to one of Plato's most significant ideas, the theory of Forms. Plato argued that things in the perceptual world were imperfect images or copies of a greater reality. Reality was not the physical world in which we lived, but rather was a realm of pure ideas, uncontaminated by material substance. Thus, the reason why a chair was a chair was because it took part in the perfect Form of the chair. In the same way, a horse was a horse because it partook of the Form of horseness. In a similar manner, particular instances of ideas such as justice and beauty were recognizable to us because we innately understood them to be representations of the perfect forms of Justice and Beauty. So, for example, a beautiful picture of a person was a less perfect copy of the person themselves. But the person's beauty is itself a reflection of the idea of beauty that we possess within our intellects. But even that concept of beauty is itself only a reflection of The Beautiful itself, the perfect form of beauty from which we are able to recognize beauty when we perceive it.

The same approach can be taken for such ideas as justice or truth. For something to be true simply means that it partakes of the metaphysical form of Truth, but in an imperfect way. Ultimately, all of these Forms themselves are simply reflections of the Good itself. The only way, Plato argues, to truly understand the nature of the reality in which we live is to dedicate one's life to the contemplation of these Forms. Most of us, however, are at best consumed by the demands of the physical and sensory world in which we live, and at worst, fascinated by the world of illusions projected at us by TV screens or computer monitors.

This idea of a division between the physical world, which is ultimately imperfect, transitory, and illusory, and the "real world" of the Forms proved to be influential throughout the ancient period. Both the Stoic philosophers and the Neo-Platonists picked up on these ideas and took them in different directions. In the same way, both Gnosticism and early Christianity were influenced by Platonic ideas. While the gnostics took up Plato's condemnation of the physical world as prison from which those with the proper knowledge could learn to escape, Christian philosophers emphasized the idea of God as the ultimate source of reality, and the physical world as participating in the Forms as created by God, and thus not wholly evil or corrupting.

ARISTOTLE

Aristotle's philosophy built on the foundation established by Socrates and Plato, but sought, as it were, to bring Plato "down to earth." While Plato's viewpoint depended on a distinction between the material world of objects and the transcendent world of the Forms, Aristotle's approach sought to embed metaphysical reality in the midst of the world we perceive.

Aristotle had been Plato's student at the Academy, although after Plato's death, he went on to establish his own school called the Lyceum. He also served for several years as the tutor of Alexander the Great, the future king of Macedonia and conqueror of the Mediterranean world. After Alexander's death, Aristotle fled Athens in fear for his life lest, he is reported to have said, "Athens sin twice against philosophy."

Aristotle's work encompasses an immense amount of territory. His lectures covered everything from logic to ethics and politics, to physics, biology, and astronomy. Along the way, he also delved into topics such as rhetoric, aesthetics, poetry, and drama. It is easy to see why he wielded such enormous influence when his work was rediscovered in the Middle Ages—there was very little in the realm of human experience that he did not address.

Among the most significant contributions that Aristotle made to philosophy was his theory of metaphysics. Unlike Plato, Aristotle understood form and matter to exist together within objects. The form of a thing does not exist in a separate realm, but rather within the world. Form, for Aristotle, described *what* a thing was, while matter was the particular instance of *this* thing versus *that* thing. Thus, we recognize two chairs as having similar characteristics that enable them to be defined as "chairs" as opposed to, say, elephants. But what distinguishes one chair from another chair is that they are not made from the same matter. Substance, for Aristotle, was the combination of form and matter.

Aristotle further argued matter and form were related to the concepts of "potentiality" and "actuality." A block of marble, for example, represents a *potential* statue. But until the sculptor applies his chisel and brings about the *form* of the statue, it is mere matter. Once it takes on form, however, it becomes an *actual* statue. Similarly, an acorn is not an oak tree, but rather a potential oak. Only when the acorn becomes an oak is its potentiality fully actualized.

Central to Aristotle's metaphysics was his theory of causes. He argued that all things were subject to four distinct causes: A *Formal Cause*, which determined what kind of thing it was (e.g., a horse, a cat, a car, a cathedral); a *Material Cause* that determined what the thing was made out of (e.g., wood, marble, steel, flesh and blood); an *Efficient Cause*, or that which brings about its form (e.g.,

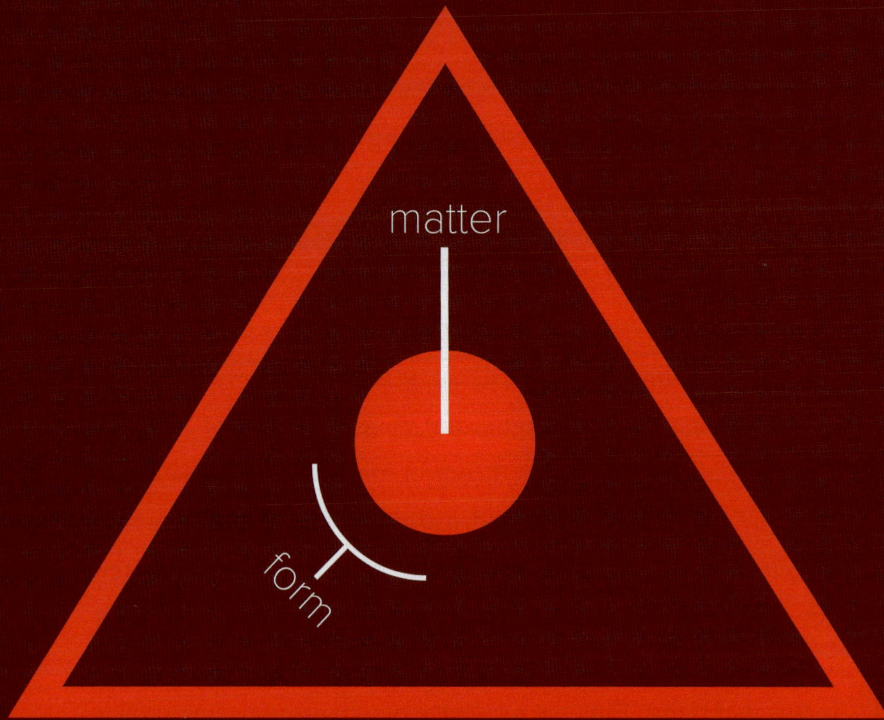

SUBSTANCE

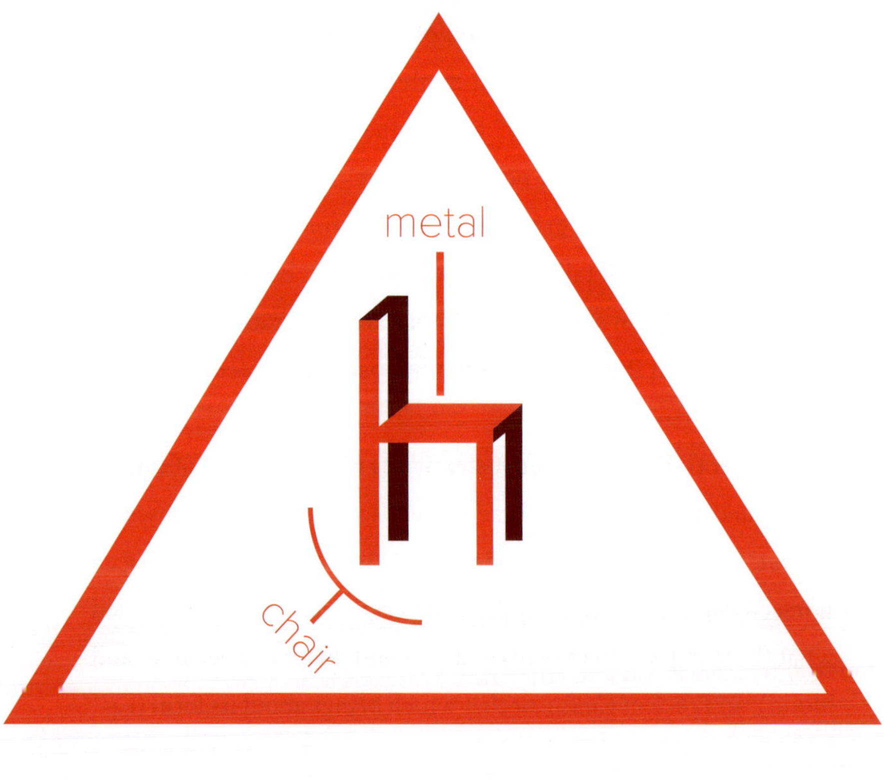

the sculptor is the efficient cause of the sculpture, the carpenter the chair, and the parents are the efficient cause of the baby); and a *Final Cause*, which defines what a thing is for, what its purpose is.

For Aristotle, nature is a *teleological* system. That is, all things within the world have a goal or purpose, a *telos*, which determines what they are for. Everything in the world is striving to increasingly embody its own perfection, determined by its purpose. The world is set in motion toward its goal of perfection by what Aristotle calls the "First Cause" or "Prime Mover." To some degree, this First Cause is a logical necessity within Aristotle's system, since it avoided the embarrassment of having to imagine an eternal regress of successive causes back to infinity. But it is also, for Aristotle, the essence of the perfection within the world. While all other things are some mixture of actuality and potentiality, and thus never fully what they strive to be, the First Cause is completely self-actualized, possessing no potentiality. The First Cause is, uniquely in the universe, fully what it is.

This teleological, or goal-oriented, approach also informed Aristotle's approach to ethics. Morality for Aristotle was concerned with the goal of human activities. Once again, unlike Plato, who understood morality as conformity to transcendent principles of justice and virtue, Aristotle began from human experience. In his *Nicomachean Ethics*, he distinguishes between the different purposes of human action. Some things we do for their own sakes, and some things we do for the sake of something else, but in either case, we act for the sake of some perceived *good*. So, for example, food and water are good because they give nourishment to the body and because of the pleasure we gain from eating and drinking. But bodily nourishment and pleasure themselves are subordinate to the ultimate good of all human activity, that of securing happiness. Happiness, however, is not good for some other purpose, but is good for its own sake. It does not exist for any other purpose than

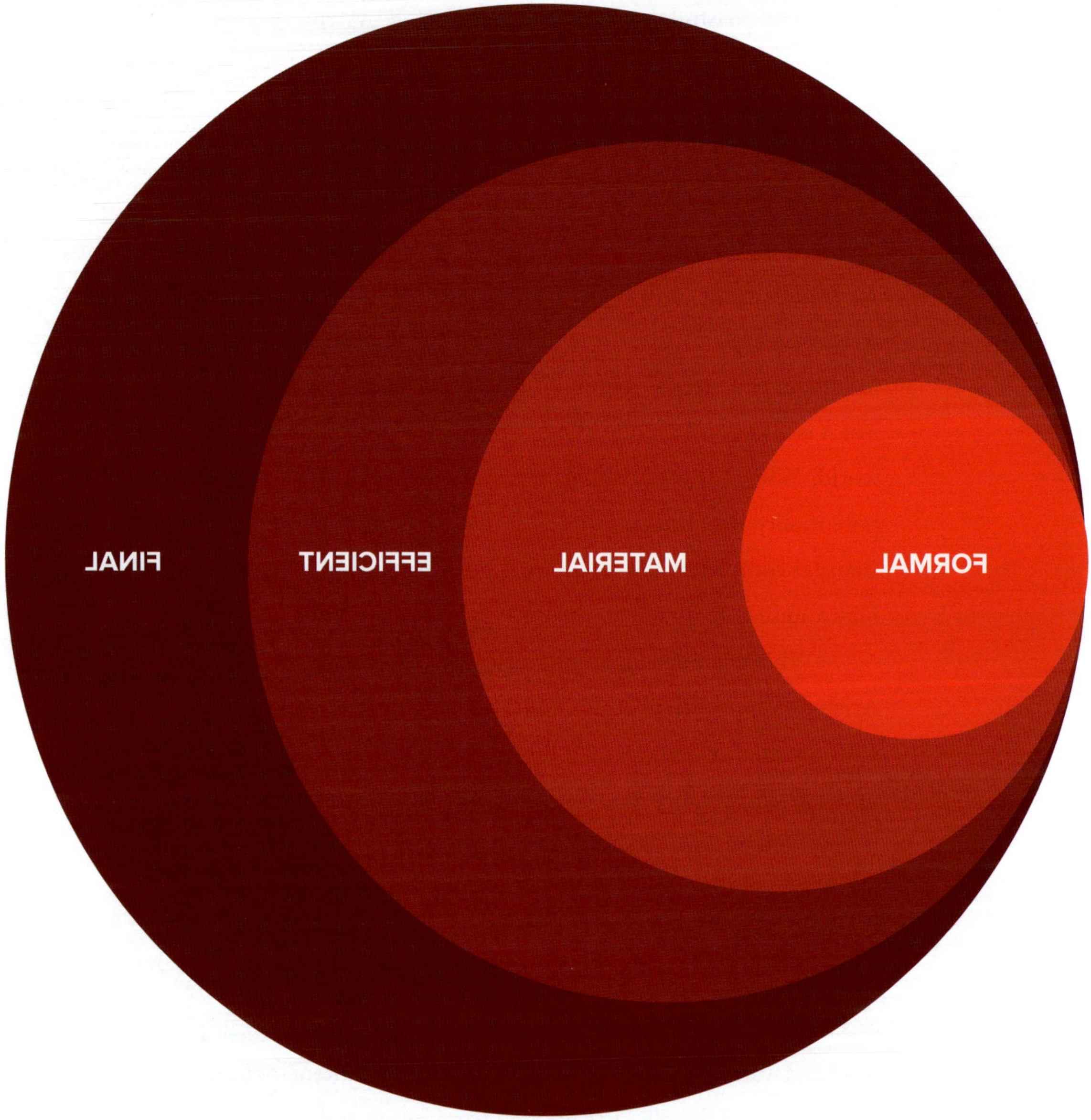
FINAL
EFFICIENT
MATERIAL
FORMAL

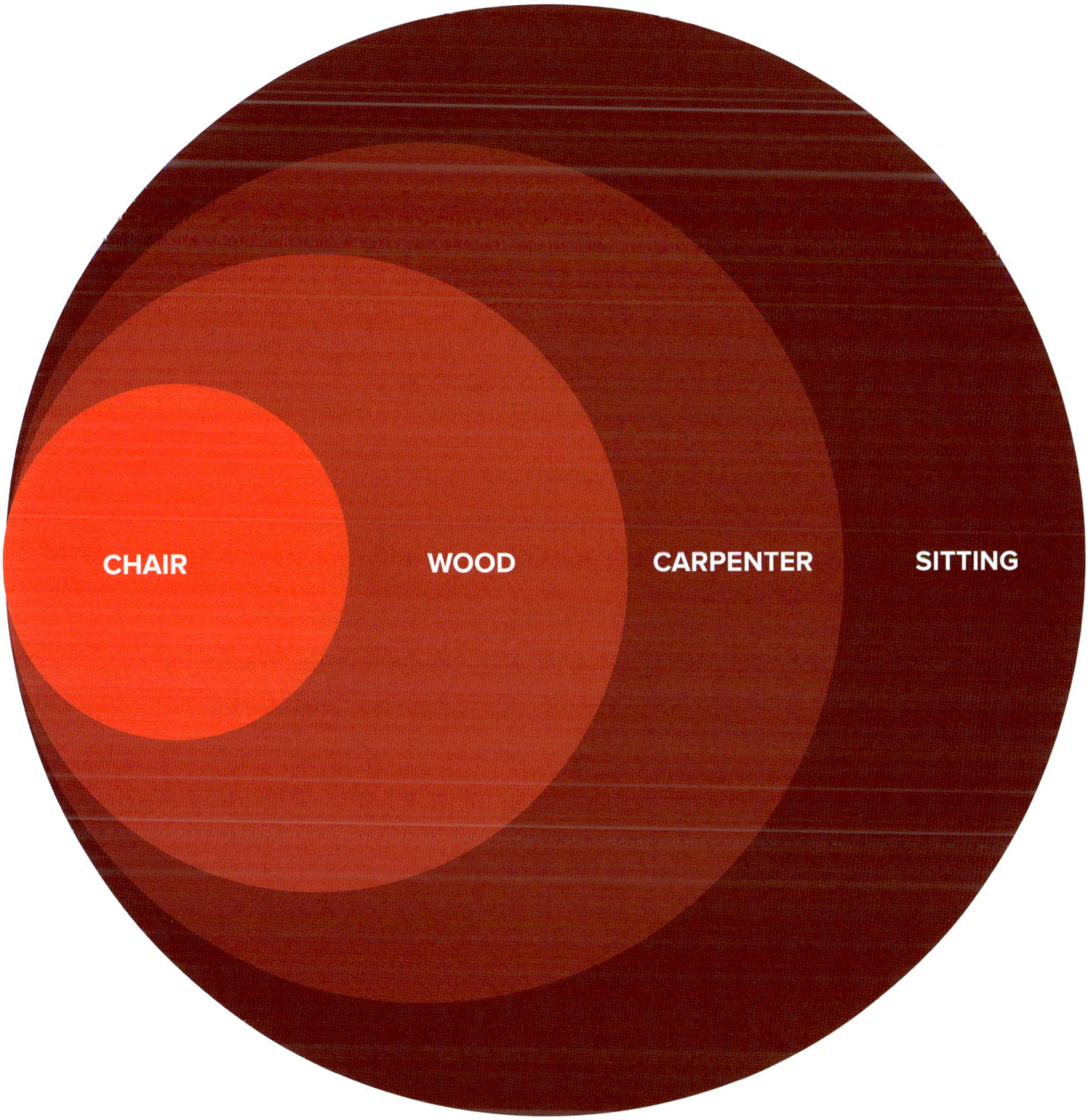

THEORY OF CAUSES

itself, and the goal of human life is to pursue those things that lead to human happiness, not just for individuals but for society as a whole (a subject that he addressed in his *Politics*). But in that case, how can we know what actions will bring us happiness? Aristotle argues that happiness is obtained through the pursuit of *virtue*.

According to Aristotle, we cannot simply *choose* to act virtuously. Virtue, he argues, is the result of practice and habit. Just as a great violinist needs years of practice to develop her skills in order to become a "virtuoso," so in order to act ethically, human beings require the cultivation of repeated practice. Virtue then becomes not a question of *choosing* between right and wrong, but simply of acting rightly as a matter of habit. Ethics is a question of developing our *character* in conformity with virtue.

But what does it mean to act virtuously? Aristotle argued that virtue was about adhering to the "golden mean"—the middle path between excess and deficiency. Courage, for example, is not the absence of fear, but rather having neither too much nor too little of it. Someone with too much fear suffers from the vice of cowardice, while someone with too little fear suffers from the vice of foolhardiness. The soldier who rushes headlong into danger is no more virtuous than the one who hides from it. It is rather the one who masters fear, is not overcome by it, and acts prudently in the face of danger who demonstrates true courage. Similarly, generosity is the mean between the extremes of greed and wastefulness, and the generous person neither hoards everything for themselves nor spends extravagantly. It is not simply giving that makes one generous, but giving wisely and prudently. Moderation, then, is at the heart of virtue.

Morality, as Aristotle argues, is a question of "practical wisdom." It is not abstract, but rooted in the concrete circumstances in which people live and act. But without practice, we will never be able to know how to respond when faced with an ethical problem.

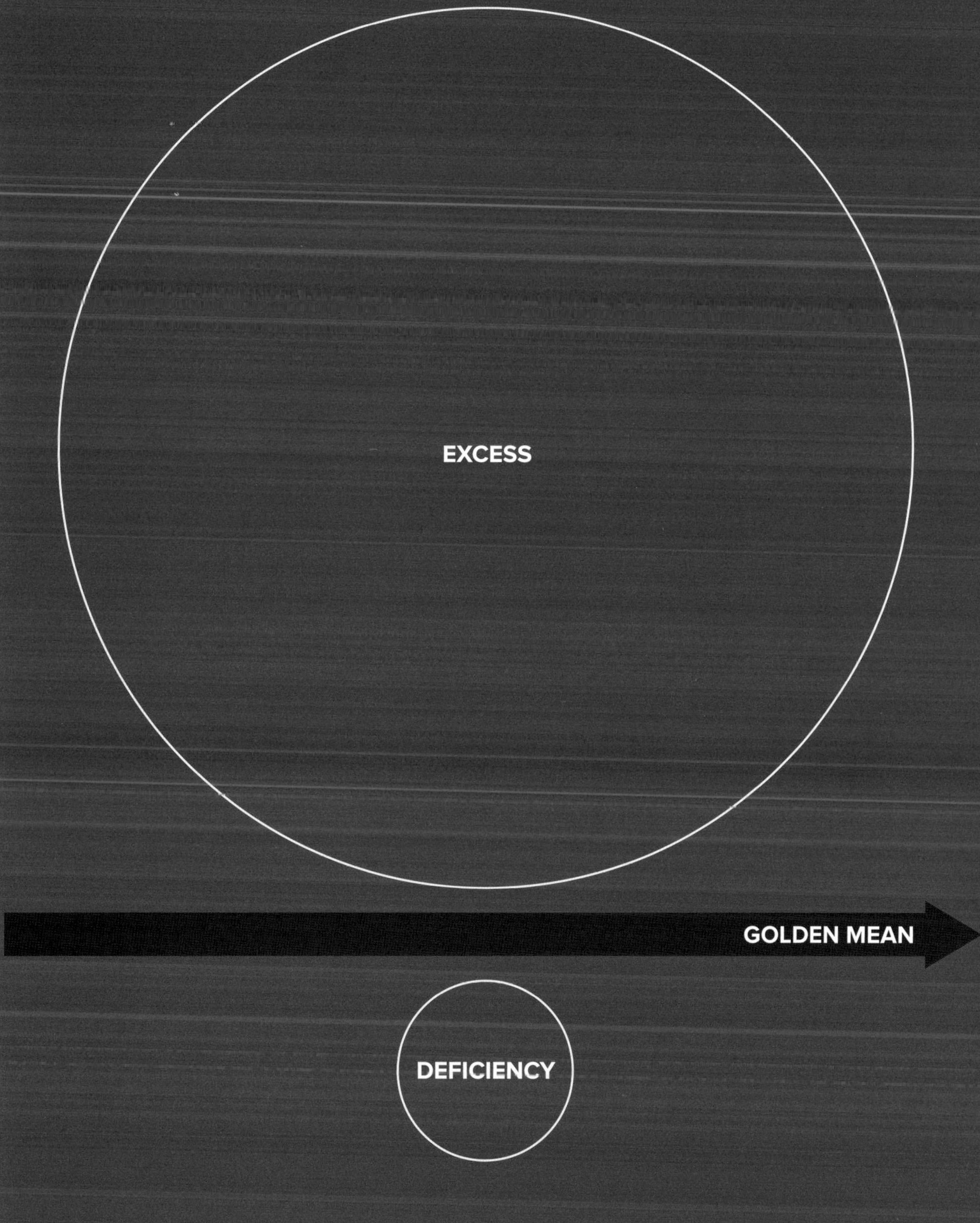
EXCESS
GOLDEN MEAN
DEFICIENCY

Even if we can intellectually distinguish between right and wrong, our habits will draw us to whatever behavior we are already disposed to, like the smoker who knows that he shouldn't have a cigarette when he first wakes up but can't stop himself because of the habit he has formed.

Happiness is ultimately the product of a life dedicated to cultivating the habits that allow us to distinguish between excess and deficiency. Human life should be dedicated to the cultivation of virtue (and thus happiness) both within ourselves and within the *polis*, or the civic realm. Thus, Aristotle argues that the happy society will be as dedicated to the cultivation of moderation and virtue as the happy individual, and the happy individual will both seek wisdom within themselves and contribute to the creation of a just and happy society.

Aristotle's works were almost entirely lost to Europe after the collapse of the Roman Empire, but were preserved in the Muslim world. One of the greatest philosophers of Islam, Muhammad ibn Rushd (called Averroës in the Western world), was also one of the great interpreters of Aristotle. His commentaries on Aristotle were influential in how he was read and interpreted by Western philosophers and theologians, particularly Thomas Aquinas. Aquinas's own theological system borrowed heavily from Aristotle, with major modifications in order to render it compatible with Christianity.

TWO

MED
IEV
AL

NOTE

There is little to distinguish the philosophy from the theology of the Middle Ages. With the formal establishment of Christianity as the religion of the Roman Empire, philosophical reflection became bound up with the theological questions explored by the burgeoning Christian faith. As the early church determined the boundaries of orthodox thought through creedal formulations such as those of Nicaea and Chalcedon, it was deeply enmeshed in philosophical as well as theological conversations. As a result, most of the major philosophical figures of Western Christianity during this period were also its major theologians.

In many ways, the theology of the medieval period arose from the need to reconcile the philosophical traditions of Platonism, Stoicism, and Aristotelianism with the biblical narratives of the Hebrew Scriptures and the New Testament. Within the Greco-Roman world, presuppositions about what it meant to speak of God, the world, matter, motion, and cause and effect were called into question by the idea that the eternal creator of the universe could be made flesh, and not even as an emperor, but a Galilean carpenter.

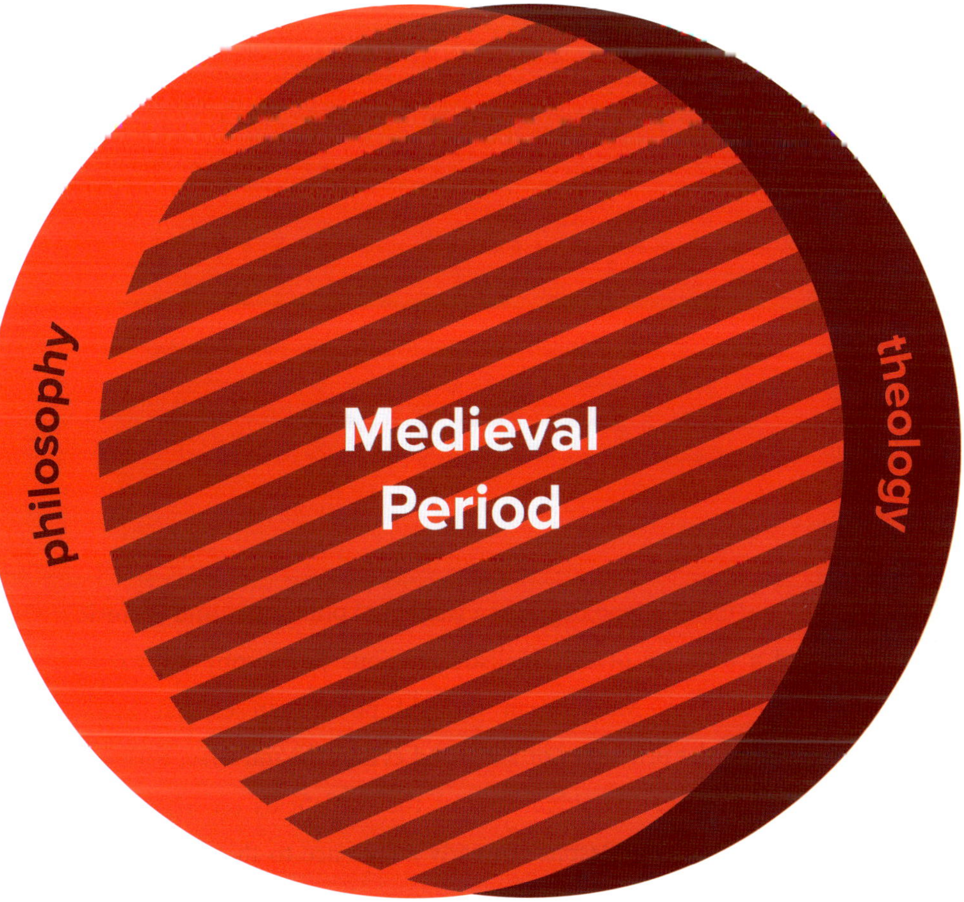
philosophy
Medieval
Period
theology

AUGUSTINE OF HIPPO

Augustine of Hippo began as a student of philosophy and rhetoric and a follower of the dualistic religious philosophy known as Manichaeism. Manichaean thought posited an eternal battle between the principles of good and evil in the universe, with the world and the individual soul as the battlefields on which that war was fought. Despite his early adherence to this philosophy, however, Augustine eventually converted to Christianity and was ultimately elevated to the position as the bishop of Hippo, in North Africa.

Central to Augustine's philosophical concerns was the question of free will. Having rejected Manichean dualism, Augustine was committed to the position that God was all-powerful; there was no cosmic counterweight to divine omnipotence. But if this was so, where did evil come from?

Good
Soul
Evil

Augustine argued that the chief error of the Manichees was in seeing evil as a *thing*, something standing in opposition to good. Augustine argued that evil was not actually a thing per se. Rather, evil was simply a lack, a privation, of good.

This "privative theory of evil" was connected to platonic metaphysics. Just as for Plato—the True, the Good, and the Beautiful were all reflections of being itself—the more good a thing was, the more real it was. God, as the ground of all existence, was the foundation of reality itself, and thus the most real thing there was. God was also the most good, and things became less good, and thus less real, the further they were from God. Ultimate evil, from this point of view, could not be said to "exist" in any genuine respect. Evil was fundamentally a lack of existence.

Because of this, we cannot shunt our responsibility for our own immorality off onto some supernatural force or creature. Rather we are ultimately responsible for our own evil acts. At the same time, Augustine insisted that our free will was tainted by the fact of original sin. We are not led to sin by some supernatural force, but rather by an inescapable inner compulsion, for which we are nevertheless responsible. Only through God's grace are we ultimately capable of escaping sin. This led Augustine into conflict with a rival theologian named Pelagius, who emphasized the freedom of the will to such a degree that he called into question the reality of original sin. He and his followers, called Pelagians, argued that human beings could live sinlessly without the aid of divine grace. In opposition to this position, Augustine argued that because our will was tainted by sin, our free will could only lead us to sin. Acting virtuously required God.

Augustine wrote on many other subjects, from biblical criticism to the theory of the just war. He tended to write in response to particular questions or controversies rather than systematically. His theology was forged in conflict, whether with

original sin

the Pelagians on free will and original sin, or with the Donatists on questions of church order and governance. In the case of the Donatists, Augustine argued that their concern for the purity of the church and the priesthood jeopardized the unity of the church. His monumental work *The City of God* offered a defense against those who blamed Christianity in the wake of the sacking of Rome. As a result of his vast corpus of writing, his thought became enormously influential and authoritative within Western Christianity. In many ways, the Protestant Reformation could be read as a story of the struggle over how best to interpret Augustine's work, as Catholic interpreters took his writings against the Donatists and in favor of church unity as the basis of their attacks on Protestants, who saw in his criticism of Pelagius a condemnation of the theology of the Roman church of their own day.

JOHN SCOTUS ERIUGENA

John Scotus Eriugena was an Irish philosopher who lived and wrote in the ninth century CE. His thought was largely derived from Neo-Platonic thought, particularly from an interpretation of the mystical text *Pseudo-Dionysius.* While this text was at Eriugena's time widely believed to have been written by Dionysius, the disciple of Paul, it has since been determined to be a non-Christian work of neoplatonist philosophy. However, due to its presumed origin, it wielded substantial influence on the philosophy and theology of the Middle Ages. Eriugena translated the work from Greek to Latin and it became foundational for his own philosophical outlook.

In his *Periphyseon*, also sometimes entitled *De Divisione Naturae* (*On the Divisions of Nature*), Eriugena divided reality into four subdivisions. The first category was that which created but was itself uncreated, a category that by definition included only God;

THE VIA POSITIVA

God is wise.

God is not ignorant.

THE VIA NEGATIVA

second were those things that both were created and create, which he calls “primordial causes”; the third were those things which were created but did not create, which he terms “created temporal effects”; and the final category was that which was uncreated and did not create, which also referred to God. The fact that God could be referred to as both creating and non-creating at first seems contradictory, but Eriugena was developing a method of discourse about God, borrowed from pseudo-Dionysius, through which God can be spoken of in often apparently contradictory ways. This is often referred to as the “via affirmativa” and the “via negativa,” or the positive way and the negative way. This was a common approach in Eastern Christianity, using the term “cataphatic” theology to refer to the positive way of coming to know God and “apophatic” theology to refer to the negative way of knowing God.

What Eriugena argues is that human language about God is by definition limited and incomplete. To say that anything *is* about God requires us also to say simultaneously that it also *is not*. God is both being in the fullest possible sense, but God is also nothing, in the sense that God utterly transcends all temporal categories of being. Being and non-being are thus related to one another, as things can be said to be in one sense and not to be in another. Because God is not a thing among other things, God’s being cannot be defined in the same categories as other beings, which exist in the realm of ordinary worldly cause and effect. Thus God both creates and does not create, in separate and distinct senses. In the first instance, all things come from God, and in the last, they all return to God.

Eriugena’s thought was of great importance to the development of subsequent philosophy in the medieval period, both insofar as he brought the work of pseudo-Dionysius to a wider audience, and via his own treatment of the positive and negative ways of coming to know God. In this respect, his influence can be felt in the theologies of Anselm of Canterbury, Peter Lombard,

uncreated creative reality (God)
primordial creative causes
created temporal effects
uncreated noncreative reality (God)

Meister Eckhardt, and Thomas Aquinas. As an interpreter of some of the key concepts of Greek mystical philosophy into a Western Christian and Latin-speaking context, he maintained an important link between the Eastern and Western churches, even after their eventual schism.

ANSELM OF CANTERBURY

Anselm of Canterbury is best known for his ontological proof for the existence of God. As formulated in his *Proslogion*, the ontological argument is a meditation on Psalm 14:1: "The fool says in his heart there is no God." Only a fool could say such a thing, Anselm states, because God's existence is self-evident.

God, he argues, exists necessarily. That is to say, God cannot *not* exist. To demonstrate this point, he argues that an object can exist in two ways—in the mind or understanding, and in reality. To exist in reality, he argues, is greater than to exist in the mind alone. God, he argues, is a being, greater than which no other being can be conceived. If God existed in our understanding alone, then we could conceive of such a being also existing in reality. However, in that case, we could conceive of a being greater than which no greater could be conceived, which would be contradictory.

Therefore, Anselm argues, since God is that than which no greater can be conceived, God must necessarily exist in reality.

He goes on to offer a second formulation of the argument, stating that God, properly understood, cannot be conceived to not exist. God is a necessary being in this sense, because God's being is not dependent on any external thing. God is unique in being *self-existent.*

This proof led to an argument between Anselm and a philosopher named Gaunilo who argued on behalf of the fool. The fact that something which exists in reality is greater than that which exists in the understanding alone does not, he argues, mean that such an object must exist. For example, he states, if I imagine the idea of a golden mountain, then a golden mountain exists in my understanding. However, that does not mean that such a thing exists in reality, however much greater the reality may be than the idea.

Anselm replies that this is true of created objects, like gold and mountains, but not of God, because necessary existence is part of God's very nature. To speak of God is to speak of a being who must necessarily exist, and so the fact that an existing God is greater in reality than in the understanding means that such a God must by definition exist.

Needless to say, this argument did not satisfy everyone, and indeed the ontological argument has been a topic of continual controversy for many centuries since, although many believe that David Hume and Immanuel Kant finally put the argument to rest by asserting that existence is not a quality of things, like color, size, and dimension. Thus it cannot be asserted as a quality of God along with the qualities of goodness, omnipotence, and omniscience. Nevertheless, Anselm's argument remains one of the central philosophical arguments in favor of God's existence.

One aspect of Anselm's thought that bears further attention is his understanding of the relationship of faith to reason. His motto, *Fides Quaerens Intellectum*, means "Faith Seeking Understanding." In his thought, faith and reason do not stand opposed to one another; rather, philosophy is the task of seeking to clarify intellectually those things that we are given by faith. Faith is inherently reasonable insofar as we are able to understand that which we believe (his other famous statement, *Credo Ut Intelligans*, means "I believe in order that I may understand"). Thus our reason may lead us more deeply into a richer faith, and enable us to comprehend ourselves and our relationship with God more fully.

THOMAS AQUINAS

To many, Thomas Aquinas represents the pinnacle of medieval philosophical thought. In his extensive corpus of theological and philosophical writing, he synthesized much of what had come before, bringing together the major insights of the ancient philosophers to which he had access (particularly Aristotle) and his theological predecessors among the church fathers, and combining them into a unified approach to understanding God, the world, and humanity. In presenting a comprehensive and systematic approach to the theology of the Western church in his own time, in such works as the *Summa Theologiae* and the *Summa Contra Gentiles* as well as his commentaries on Aristotle, he set the philosophical and theological agenda for the remainder of the Middle Ages.

The single most significant influence on Aquinas's philosophical approach was the rediscovery of Aristotle's writings in the twelfth century. Prior to this, Aristotle's work was only available in fragmentary form in the West. However, after Arabic translations were brought back from the Middle East during the crusades, his work once again began to be widely translated, discussed, and analyzed. Aristotle's rejection of a personal God was a problematic aspect of his philosophy, and one that theologians had to overcome in their use of him. Thomas opened the door for the widespread adoption of Aristotle's entire body of work to the Western Christian world, and it eventually came to predominate theological discourse in the later Middle Ages.

Aquinas's thought, like Aristotle's, covered a vast array of material, from metaphysics to nature, human morality, politics, and society, and of course God. However, two areas where his thought has been of enduring interest have been his exploration of the relationship of faith and reason and his "five ways" of proving God's existence.

Thomas argued that faith and reason are not contradictory to one another, but rather that they are different ways of viewing the same phenomena. Philosophy examines things from the perspective of reason, while theology does so within the realm of faith. Properly done, the answers of these two disciplines do not contradict one another, nor are the discoveries of theology contrary to reason. Reason, unaided by revelation, can discover a great deal about the nature of the universe and our place in it, such as the nature of matter and motion, principles of morality, and even the existence of God. On the other hand, reason cannot establish those things that we come to know through revelation. Philosophy can establish the truth of the world in a way that is consistent with the insights of theology. However, not everything that theology affirms can be established solely within philosophy.

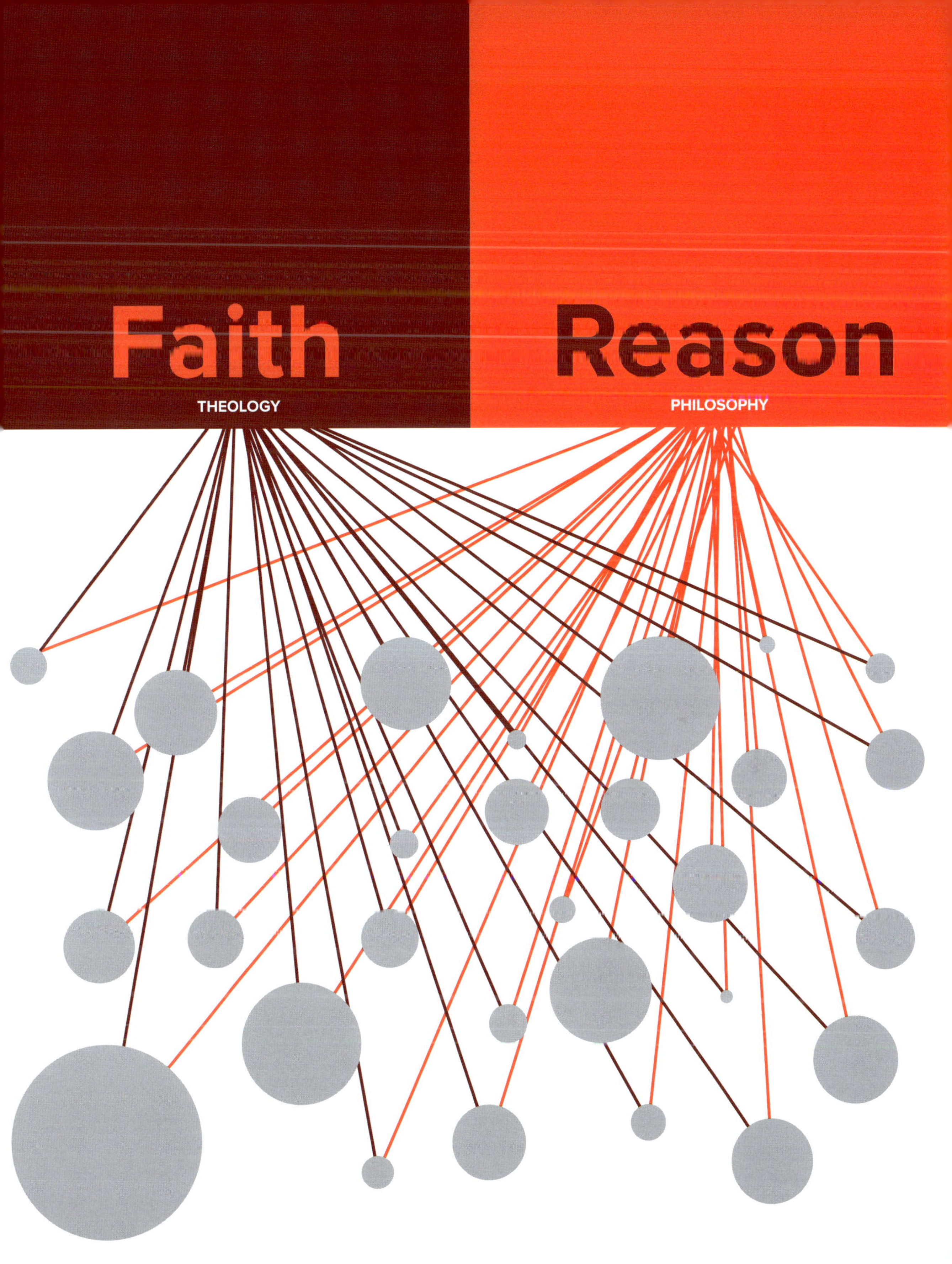
Faith
THEOLOGY
Reason
PHILOSOPHY

Some theological propositions (such as the triune nature of God or Jesus Christ as the incarnation of the Second Person of the Trinity) can be accepted only on the basis of revelation. This does not mean that they are *irrational*, but only that their truth cannot be established on the basis of reason itself. These things are believed to be true on the basis of faith and we reason about them based on that starting point. Philosophy and theology are different ways of knowing about the same reality.

This is exemplified in Aquinas's five ways of proving the existence of God in the *Summa Theologiae*. Reason, he argues, can establish the fact that God must exist, though it cannot demonstrate many of the salient characteristics of God that are specific to the Christian faith, for example, that God is triune or became incarnate in Jesus Christ. Borrowing his core principle from Aristotle's metaphysics, Aquinas attempts to establish God's existence via reason alone. Each of Aquinas's five arguments is interlocked with the others. Aquinas begins with the idea that God can be known by virtue of God's effects within the natural world. In the first instance, he argues, following Aristotle, God can be known as the First Mover. All things that move must be moved in their turn by something else; there must be a being to begin the process, or else there would be an infinite regress of cause and effect, which Aquinas believed to be contradictory. In a related argument, Aquinas asserts that no thing can be the efficient cause of itself, and therefore God must exist as the primal efficient cause of all things. In a third argument, he states that things can only come into being from nothingness by virtue of something that exists by necessity—in other words, God. His fourth argument asserts that it is only possible to establish things as better or worse than one another on the basis of some idea of what is best or greatest, and God is the name we give for that which is source of that which is good and perfect in all things. His final argument is based on the

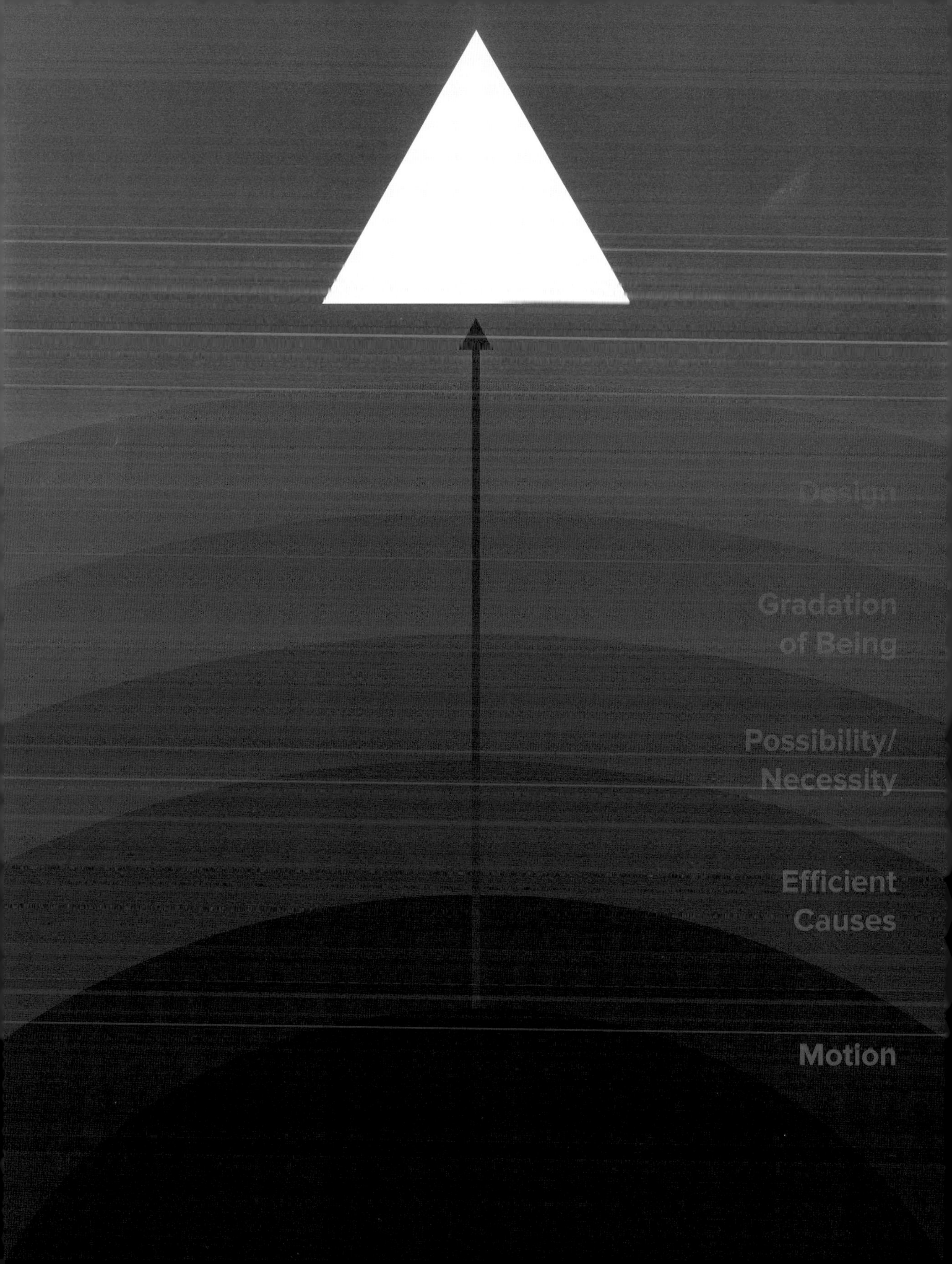
Design
Gradation of Being
Possibility/ Necessity
Efficient Causes
Motion

idea that all things, even those that do not act with intelligence or intention, act toward some goal or end, and God is the proper end toward which all natural things gravitate.

Unlike Anselm's ontological argument, Aquinas's five ways are all rooted in an inference from the created world to the existence of God. Like other attempts to rationally establish God's existence, these arguments have been called into serious question in the modern era. Nevertheless, they have retained an enormous degree of staying power and persuasiveness, particularly within the realm of Catholic theology and philosophy. Note, however, that Aquinas's arguments do not establish anything *in particular* about the nature of the God whose existence he claims to have proven, except that God must in some way function as a primordial cause of all things, and must have necessary being as part of the divine nature. In other words, his proofs attempt to establish that God is the perfect and self-existent creator of all things, but say nothing about the question of whether God is best known through the teachings of the Christian, or any other, faith. In this sense, it is purely philosophical. However, as Aquinas attempts to establish the truth of the elements of Christian faith elsewhere in the *Summa*, he continually reaffirms that nothing that the Christian faith teaches is contrary to the nature of God as we come to know it through reason alone, nor is reason capable of establishing anything about the nature of God, which is contrary to the Christian faith. Philosophy and theology thus have a complimentary and supporting relationship to one another.

Modern philosophy, beginning with René Descartes, would call that complementarity into question.

THREE

RATIO NAL ISM

RENÉ DESCARTES

René Descartes is generally considered to be the first modern philosopher, as well as the founder of the philosophical movement that came to be known as "rationalism." The core of rationalist philosophy, as we will observe, is that genuine knowledge about the world can only be achieved through the application of rational thought, rather than through our senses. Our senses, after all, can be deceived, but the rationalists believed that our minds were capable of arriving at certainty about the nature of ourselves and the world, as well as the nature and attributes of God.

Descartes was born in France and had early ambitions to become a military officer. A series of mystical visions, however, convinced him to change his course to the study of philosophy, science, and mathematics, where he did groundbreaking work in geometry, in addition to developing a heliocentric model of the

il falloit néces-
sairement que
moi qui le pen-
sois fusse
quelque chose;
et remarquant
que cette
vérité, **i think,**
therefore I am,
étoit si ferme
et si assurée

René Descartes, *Discours de la Méthode,* Part IV

solar system around the same time as Galileo Galilei (which he prudently filed away after hearing of Galileo's arrest for developing a similar system).

Descartes wrote extensively in philosophy. His best-known work, *Meditations on First Philosophy*, attempted to establish a firm foundation for human knowledge by reflecting first on his own experience of the world. This is often referred to as the "subjective turn" and represents a distinct departure from the approach to knowledge represented by medieval philosophy. Descartes's question was "How can we arrive at certainty about the world?" whereas the central question of medieval philosophy was "How can faith and reason be reconciled?"

The *Meditations* is constructed as a series of short essays, through which Descartes first attempts to call into doubt everything he knows about the external world, and then, he hopes, to reestablish knowledge on the basis of that which he finds impossible to doubt. He attempts to doubt anything and everything that he can conceivably doubt. He argues that we can never be absolutely certain of the evidence of our senses, since they are fallible and prone to mislead us. He asks if it is possible to doubt whether he is actually sitting in front of his fire writing. Recalling that, on other occasions, he's believed himself to be doing just that only to wake up and discover it was a dream, he concludes that he can indeed doubt it. It's always *possible* that he could be dreaming, even if it is unlikely.

He then goes on to ask whether he can doubt the truths of mathematics. Could he, for example, doubt that 2 + 2 = 4? Since it seems that mathematical truth ought to be as certain as anything could be, it seems hard to doubt; but he asks, what if, instead of a benevolent God, the universe is instead run by an evil demon? A good God wouldn't deceive us about the truths of math, but an evil demon might. So again, it is *possible* to doubt even the truth of mathematics.

It's important to bear in mind that Descartes does not claim to genuinely believe these things. He doesn't really believe he's dreaming at a given moment, or that the universe is run by an evil demon. Rather, his claim is that it is impossible to be *absolutely certain* that these things are not the case. Our senses *may* not be deceiving us, but they could be. We *may* not be dreaming, but it is possible we are. The universe probably *is not* run by an evil demon, but we cannot prove, at least at this point, that it is not. So the absence of certainty is, for Descartes, sufficient grounds to doubt it entirely. It is an *intellectual* doubt rather than an *existential* doubt.

Nevertheless, having arrived at a state in which he has no way of trusting his senses, and no way of knowing for certain whether he's awake, dreaming, or the plaything of an evil demon, Descartes begins to wonder if there is anything that he can know for certain. At this point, he arrives at the phrase for which he is best known, concluding that in the absence of any other certainty, there is still *one thing* that it is impossible for him to doubt: his own existence. "I am. I exist," he writes. Elsewhere he gives this idea its more famous formulation: "I think, therefore I am" (*cogito ergo sum*). Even if nothing else is true of the world, the fact that it is he thinking about these things is the one irreducible certainty in the universe.

Having established with certainty his own existence as a thinking thing, Descartes still has to determine how it is possible to believe in anything else. His next step is to examine the furniture of his mind. There, he finds a concept of an infinite, benevolent God, which he argues he could not, as a finite creature, have created himself. Since the only creature capable of creating such a concept must itself be an infinite creature, Descartes argues (using a version of the ontological argument developed independently of St. Anselm), that such an infinite, benevolent God must necessarily exist.

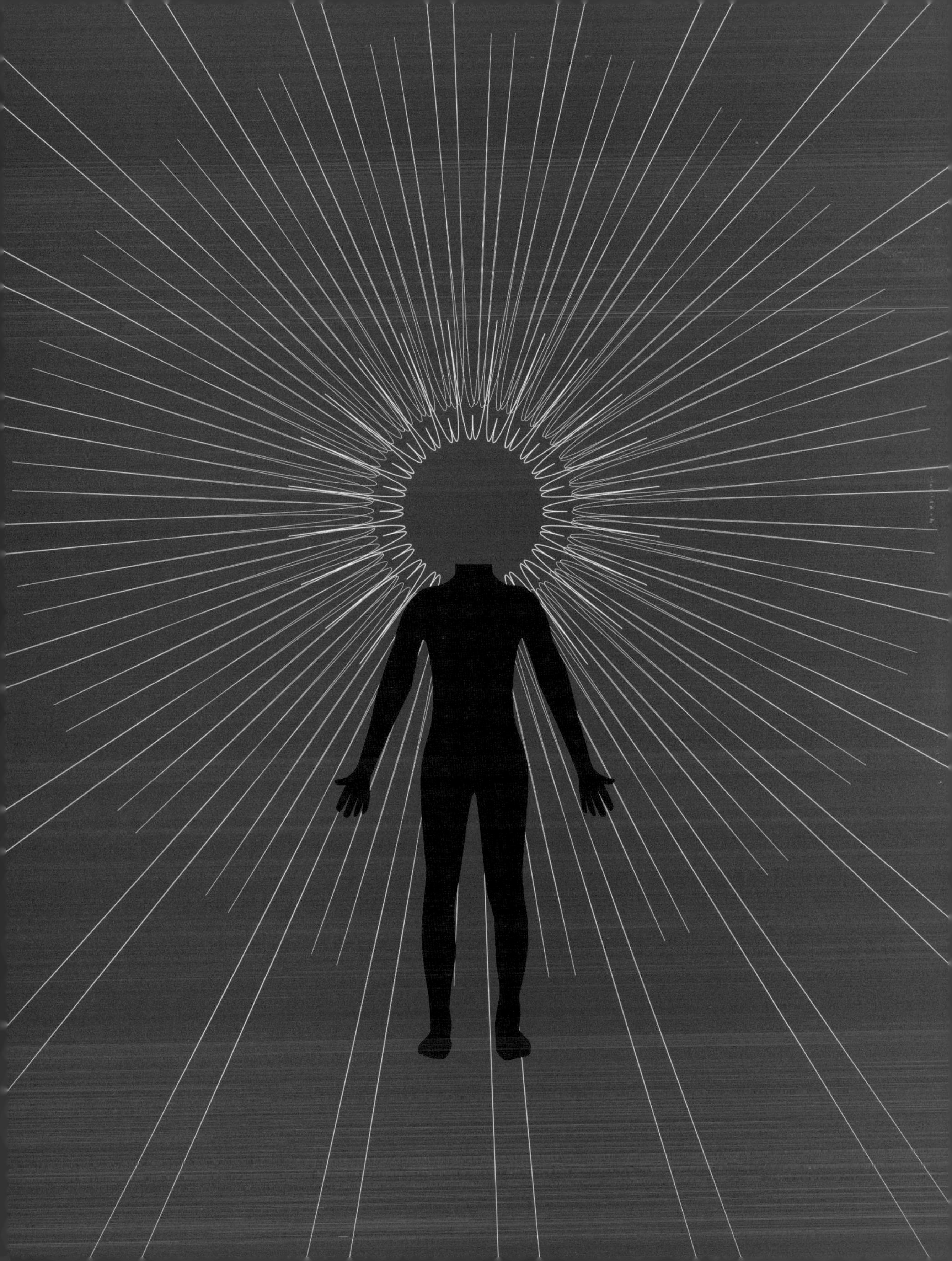

Having established the existence of himself as a thinking thing, a mind, and the existence of an all-powerful, infinite, benevolent God, he then reestablishes the existence of the external, material world, arguing that, since a benevolent God would not deceive him, it is possible to deduce the truths of the material world on the basis of his sense perception. In this way, Descartes believes, he has established a basis for genuine and certain knowledge of the world. In doing so, Descartes sets a new trajectory for philosophy as well as for theology, away from reliance on traditional authority and toward the reliance on reason alone to establish truth about both God and the world.

Subsequent philosophical work would be done directly in response to the path blazed by Descartes, either by building on or critiquing his project. However, Descartes also created a number of quandaries, particularly for theology. Whereas in the Middle Ages the soul and the body had been seen as distinct yet inseparable parts of the human being, Descartes established a strong division between mind and body. In the same vein, by insisting that philosophy should be built on the rational, subjective experience of the knower, he—intentionally or not—undermined arguments from authority that had been the basis for much Christian doctrine up to that point. In conjunction with the Protestant Reformation, this change in the way that philosophy was done seriously undermined the role of the church in the intellectual life of Europe. Philosophers after Descartes no longer sought to root their thought in the context of the church's teachings. On the contrary, theology more and more began to adjust itself to philosophical fashion, often to its own detriment.

BARUCH SPINOZA

Benedict (or Baruch) Spinoza was raised within the Sephardic Jewish community in Amsterdam, although by his early twenties he had abandoned most of the central tenets of Judaism. In 1556, he was expelled from the synagogue on the grounds of heresy. His most prominent philosophical writings, particularly his *Ethics* and his *Tractatus Theologico-Philosophicus*, certainly contained ideas that outraged more traditional religious thinkers in both Judaism and Christianity. His metaphysical conclusions were far more radical than Descartes's, particularly with regard to his view of God, but just as scandalous at the time was his approach to reading the Bible, as he was among the first to treat the Bible not as an inspired text but as a historical document.

Many philosophers have admired the order and structure of Euclid's *Geometry*, but nobody took that admiration to quite the degree that Spinoza did. Inspired by Euclid's deductive method—moving from definitions, to axioms, to corollaries in order to offer mathematically sound proofs of his propositions—Spinoza attempted to build his *Ethics* on a similar basis. Thus the book reads very differently than most other works of philosophy. Like Euclid, he attempted to derive his conclusions deductively from what he viewed to be self-evident premises.

Descartes had argued that the universe was ultimately constituted by three kinds of substance: God (an infinite benevolent being), mind (the self as a thinking thing), and matter (extension in space). Spinoza goes further, arguing that there is ultimately only one substance in the universe, and that substance is God. Mind and matter are not substances apart from God, but are rather attributes of that singular substance. In effect, Spinoza argues, God is identical with nature. As a result of this position, Spinoza was generally considered to be (and condemned as) a pantheist.

This identification of God and nature has several implications for Spinoza's philosophy. In the first place, Spinoza views God not in the traditional Jewish or Christian sense as a being with will or intention who acts for the sake of bringing the world to a particular goal or outcome. While God is the active principle of nature (*Natura naturans*), God is not an agent. Rather, the world is produced and sustained by that active principle (*Natura naturata*). Additionally, since God is identical to nature, Spinoza denies the possibility of miracles, arguing that all phenomena in the world are the result of natural cause and effect.

Mind and matter, Spinoza argued, are attributes of this singular substance, and not ultimately separable either from one another or from God. In one sense, this solves the problem that Descartes had stumbled into in his own metaphysics by arguing that mind and body were separate substances, thus raising the question of how they interacted with one another. Descartes's

GOD DEUS
OR SIVE
NATURE NATURA
SPINOZA

solution, perplexingly, was to argue that they met in the pineal gland of the brain; Spinoza's solution is more elegant, in that he argues that, as attributes of the same, infinite substance, they are innately connected to one another.

Further, since God, mind, matter, and nature are all identical, just as there are no miracles, there is not really any such thing as free will in the sense of autonomous, undetermined choice. Rather, human action is the result of the same system of cause and effect as the rest of the natural world. Ethical action, then, is not about choosing the right path between moral obstacles, but about developing the right attitude toward our place within the natural world. Our goal, he argues, should be to free ourselves of our passions and strive for what he calls a state of "blessedness," which he views as being embodied by a constant desire to increase in our knowledge of God and our relationship to God. In many ways, Spinoza's approach to both theology and ethics was reminiscent of the ancient Stoic philosophers.

In his *Tractatus Theologico-Politicus* (*Theological-Political Treatise*), Spinoza turned his philosophical analysis to the interpretation of the Bible and the proper organization of society. Building on the work of Moses Maimonides and Thomas Hobbes, Spinoza engaged in a rigorous critique of the Bible, arguing that it should be read as a historical text, and as such, was as liable to error as any other human product. The importance of the Bible is in its moral message rather than in the infallible truth of its words or the factual status of its narrative. Spinoza denied, for example, that Moses wrote the whole of the Pentateuch. At the heart of it, the Bible teaches love of neighbor and obedience to God. Philosophy should not be subject to theology, he argues. Rather they are two completely separate fields. Religious authorities and precepts do not offer a privileged path to God, but are artifacts of the time and place that they were created. Religions are an imaginative expression of God. Thus, Spinoza rejects the Jewish ritual and ceremonial law in which he was raised as irrelevant and superfluous to his day and age, arguing that they applied only to the ancient Israelite kingdom. Philosophy, he argues, should be free from religious interference.

As to the state, Spinoza argues in a manner similar to Hobbes; the state exists to control the tendency toward egoism that humans display in the state of nature. The sovereign, he argues, has an obligation to oversee all aspects of public life in society, including religious organization and ritual. Spinoza believed, however, that private religious belief should be left to the individual, as matters of personal piety did not affect the ability of the sovereign to rule.

Spinoza's philosophy, particularly his approach to the Bible and to political life, wielded a substantial influence on subsequent philosophers. Social contract theorists, such as John Locke and Jean-Jacques Rousseau, would build on the work of Spinoza and Hobbes in the development of democratic political theory. In the nineteenth century, biblical scholars such as Gotthold Lessing and Wilhelm Dilthey would build on his approach to the Bible, paving the way for the creation of modern biblical scholarship. Spinoza's metaphysical work would contribute to the further development of rationalist philosophy, and the torch of that movement would be taken up by G. W. Leibniz.

G. W. LEIBNIZ

Gottfried Wilhelm Leibniz was the third of the great rationalist philosophers. Born in Leipzig in 1646, he distinguished himself as a philosopher, mathematician, scientist, and diplomat. In mathematics, he is best known for having invented calculus at the same time as Sir Isaac Newton, which led the two of them to a bitter, years-long debate about who had done so first. His best-known philosophical works, *Monadology* and *Theodicy*, deal with questions of metaphysics and the problem of evil, respectively. The second work may be best known today as being the centerpiece of Voltaire's satirical novel *Candide*, which repeatedly (and unfairly) skewers Leibniz's dictum that this is the "best of all possible worlds."

Leibniz builds on the groundwork laid by Descartes and Spinoza in the construction of his own metaphysical system, but whereas Descartes had argued that there were three substances

MONADS ARE SIMPLE

(mind, matter, and God), and Spinoza had argued that there was just one (God), Leibniz argues that there are an infinite number of substances, which he terms "monads." Monads are eternal, indivisible, individual, and "windowless"; that is to say, they do not interact with one another. Rather, each monad possesses within itself a reflection of the entire universe. Monads relate to one another through what Leibniz calls a "pre-established harmony." In other words, while the various individual aspects of the world (people, trees, stars, planes, trains, and automobiles) may *seem* to be continually interacting with one another, in fact they have no direct connection. Rather, they are metaphysically joined so that the entire universe operates as a unity. Whereas Descartes had argued that matter was a substance alongside mind, Leibniz's monads consisted only of mind. Matter was a phenomenon (that is, something perceived), but not a substance in itself. (This is an idea we will encounter again when we look at the empiricism of George Berkeley.) Since monads constitute the entirety of reality, this means that everything in the universe in some way can be considered a "mind," although nothing interacts directly with anything else. According to Leibniz, all things ultimately emanate, in a way reminiscent of neoplatonism, from God, who experiences the world from the perspective of all monads simultaneously, and serves as the basis for the establishment of the harmony among all of the monads within the universe.

It is important to note that while Leibniz's theory of monads bears some resemblance to the atomic theory of philosophers like Epicurus and Lucretius, as well as the later atomic theory that became the basis for modern science, he is arguing something different. There is a *sense* in which all things are made of monads, just as in atomic theory all things are made of atoms. But on a deeper level, Leibniz is actually arguing that all things *are* monads. So while, for example, atomic theory would say that my desk, my computer, and I are all made up of atoms, Leibniz would go further, arguing that we all, in fact, both are made of monads and *are* monads. In other words, monads aren't simply the component parts that make up the world—they are all of the individual things in the world as well. I am a monad, and I am made of monads. All of these monads individually carry the entirety of the world within them in a form of pre-established harmony.

Far more influential than his monadology, however, is Leibniz's approach to grappling with the problem of evil. In *Théodicée* (which means "God's justice"), Leibniz attempts to argue for the goodness of God in spite of the reality of evil in the world. Leibniz's argument is complex and often misunderstood. It is often assumed (largely thanks to Voltaire) that in arguing that we live in the best of all possible worlds, Leibniz is arguing that there is no real evil in the world, but only the appearance of evil. But this is not the case. Leibniz accepts the reality of evil, but argues that one can rationally believe in a benevolent God nevertheless, because it is *possible* that God, being omnipotent, omniscient, and benevolent, possesses the capacity to view all possible universes at once, determining which possible universes would have the greatest balance of good over evil on the whole.

Leibniz argues that, if this world were not the best possible world, then that would imply that God was not omniscient, not omnipotent, or not benevolent. But since the nature of God (using another version of Anselm's ontological argument) is by definition omniscient, omnipotent, and benevolent, that cannot be the case. Furthermore, since God's goal is to bring about the most perfect possible world, if it were possible for a better world to have been created, then God would have created that world instead. Thus, despite the unquestionable existence of genuine and often horrific evil, Leibniz argues, this world is the best one possible.

One important point to note is that Leibniz, at least in the *Theodicy*, does not present this as an ironclad proof. Rather, Leibniz is attempting to demonstrate that religious belief is *rational* when it can be shown to be consistent and coherent. If one's beliefs are not self-contradictory, then it is not necessary to *prove* their truth in order to believe them rationally. One only needs to provide a possible explanation to account for objections. While there were those who argued (as they do today) that the existence of evil contradicts the possibility of an omnipotent, omniscient, and benevolent God, Leibniz argued that there was nothing *innately* contradictory about it. Rather, it could rationally be the case that God brought into being the only world where the balance of good outweighed evil, and in offering an explanation for how such a situation might be possible, Leibniz was attempting to demonstrate the rationality of belief.

Needless to say, Leibniz did not put the problem of evil to rest, any more than he put the problems of metaphysics to rest. Nevertheless, his philosophy remains important largely because of his contribution to what came to be known as the "greater good" argument in debates about the problem of evil, in which evil is justified on the basis of some greater good which it serves. While this was not the entirety of Leibniz's argument, it remains common, as do critiques of it. Furthermore, Leibniz's philosophy serves as an important precursor to the philosophy of Immanuel Kant. However, before we can turn to him we need to consider the other major stream of modernist philosophical tradition, known as empiricism.

FOUR

EMPIRICISM

JOHN LOCKE

Empiricism represents the major alternative to rationalism in seventeenth- and eighteenth-century philosophy. While rationalism was more influential in continental Europe during this period, empiricism was much more influential in Great Britain and its English-speaking colonies. Whereas rationalism was intent on rooting knowledge in clear and distinct ideas of the mind, apart from our perceptions of the world, empiricism took the opposite approach, seeking to understand the world, first and foremost, by means of our senses.

John Locke was the first of the great empiricist philosophers. A physician by training, he distinguished himself not only in the philosophy of knowledge, but also in political theory, carving new ground in both economics and government. Additionally, he was an early proponent of religious toleration in England, and

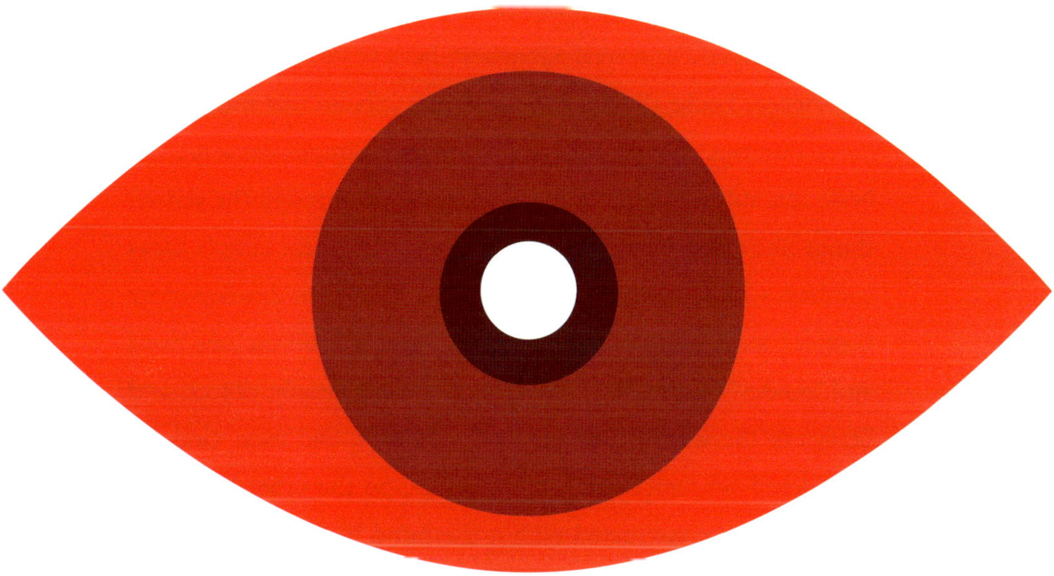

his support of religious freedom was deeply influential on, among many others, Thomas Jefferson.

In his *Essay Concerning Human Understanding*, Locke argued—against Descartes—that the human mind does not come pre-furnished with ideas of any kind. Rather, the mind is a "blank slate," on which we draw throughout our lives through sense experience. We are born with no innate ideas but construct the world piecemeal as we come into contact with it. We know that no such ideas exist, he argues, because there is nothing that all human beings universally hold to be true. Even things that seem to demand universal agreement have to be learned through experience. Locke divides the ideas that inhabit our minds into two categories: simple and complex ideas. Simple ideas are the basic sensations that enter our consciousness through the senses, things like color, sound, sensation, and taste. These simple ideas combine within our minds in order to enable us to develop more complex ideas, about what he calls "substances" on the one hand and "modes" on the other. Substances are, essentially, objects and beings in the world. Humans, rocks, houses, and even God are considered substances by Locke. Modes, on the other hand, are ideas that are constructed within the mind itself, such as moral precepts or mathematical concepts. A third category Locke addresses is what he calls "relations," specifically the relationship between substances and modes. Thus, unlike the rationalists, Locke believes that our knowledge is, as it were, constructed from the ground up. We decorate the blank slate of our consciousness with experience and thus come to understand the world one step at a time.

Another distinction Locke makes, borrowed from Galileo and Thomas Boyle, is between what he terms "primary" and "secondary" qualities of objects in the world. Primary qualities are things like shape, size, dimension, location, and motion. They

Let us then suppose the mind to be, as we say, white paper, void of all characters, without any ideas: — How comes it to be furnished?...
Experience.

Let us then suppose the mind to be, as we say, **white paper,** void of all characters, without any ideas: — How comes it to be furnished?...

Experience.

John Locke, Essay Concerning Human Understanding, II.1.2

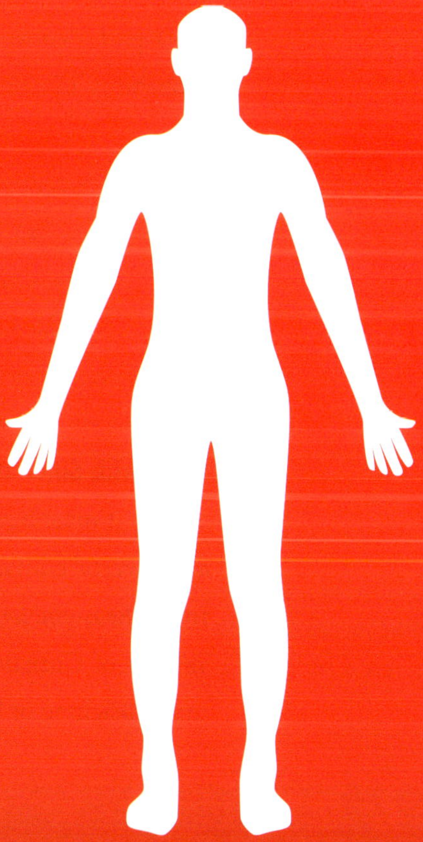

describe the physical qualities of objects in space. Secondary qualities are things like color, scent, taste, and sound. These are qualities through which we come to perceive objects but which are not innate to objects themselves. Secondary qualities of objects are what produce ideas in our consciousness. We come to perceive the primary qualities of objects only through our encounter with their secondary qualities. Underlying all of these qualities, primary and secondary, are what Locke calls "material substance."

Because our ideas are formed from sense perceptions, Locke argues that we can never know most things with complete certainty. Like Descartes, Locke believed we can be certain of our own existence, and we can infer the existence of God and certain logical and mathematical concepts with certainty but, apart from that, we can have no genuine certainty of the world. In this regard, Locke isn't as far from Descartes as he might appear, but while the rationalists sought to find certain knowledge in clear and distinct ideas, Locke believed such an objective was pointless. For the most part, "knowledge" was just a word we use to describe the probability of something being one way rather than another. By virtue of our senses we can know some things about the world with a high degree of certainty, and other things with somewhat less certainty, but very little with complete confidence.

Of particular interest in Locke's account is his argument that it is possible to determine the existence of God on the basis of an empiricist conception of knowledge. He infers God's existence, not from any innate idea of God, but rather from the existence of the world. Since the world cannot have come from nothing, he argues, it must have been created by an eternal, all-knowing, and all-powerful entity, whether or not we prefer to call that entity God. In *The Reasonableness of Christianity*, he defended a non-dogmatic version of Christianity, based on the Bible and focusing on the moral teaching of Jesus Christ rather than on complex speculative theological doctrines. Locke's own theology reflected this view. He rejected the doctrine of the Trinity and the idea of Christ as the eternal Son of God, emphasizing that Christianity only required the acceptance of Jesus as the messiah. In this respect, he was very much involved in the seventeenth-century debates about the necessity of traditional theological principles to Christian belief. While he remained a member of the Church of England all of his life, he shared an unorthodox approach to theology with a number of his contemporary philosophical and scientific peers, most notably Isaac Newton. At the same time, he was deeply suspicious of what he termed "enthusiasm," which he believed abandoned reason for the sake of faith. Whatever the truth of Christianity might be, Locke argued, it could only be understood by the use of our reason. Given his insistence that our beliefs must ultimately be rooted in our experience of the sensible world, his resistance to both what he would have seen as speculative theological concepts and what he would have seen as irrationalism is understandable.

Perhaps because of his unorthodox theological beliefs, Locke was also concerned to make the case for religious tolerance. In his *Letter Concerning Toleration*, he argues that religious belief should be a matter of individual conscience rather than a matter of law. In the wake of the Protestant Reformation, the Wars of Religion, and the religious turmoil that had affected the English church during that period, Locke argued that religion was a fundamentally private affair and that belief could not be compelled by the threat of punishment. At the same time, Locke's toleration did not extend to atheists, who he argued were fundamentally untrustworthy and incapable of acting from genuinely moral motivations.

GEORGE BERKELEY

George Berkeley picked up where John Locke left off, further developing and expanding the core ideas of empiricism, pressing them further than Locke had been willing to. Berkeley studied at Trinity College in Dublin and was ordained in the Anglican Church. He was well acquainted with the currents of modern philosophy and science and kept extensive notebooks of his own philosophical reflections, which emerged from his study of Descartes, Locke, Newton, and many others. He returned to teach at Trinity, and was eventually made Bishop of Cloyne, in Ireland. His most well-known work, *Three Dialogues Between Hylas and Phylonous*, is an encapsulation of his philosophy, which rejects materialism and embraces a form of metaphysical idealism.

The two main characters of the *Dialogues* represent alternative approaches to metaphysics. Hylas, whose name derives from the Greek word for "matter," advocates for the existence of material substance, while Philonous, whose name means "mind-lover," advocates for Berkeley's idealism. Over the course of their conversation, each attempts to convince the other of the validity of his own viewpoint, though in the end, perhaps predictably, Philonous prevails.

Berkeley begins, as Locke did, by arguing that the sole source of human knowledge is sense perception. We are only permitted to affirm that which our senses can establish, or which we can validly infer from sense data. He argues that since we experience the world solely by means of perception, we can only know about what we perceive. However, he goes on to argue, we do not perceive *material* objects. Rather, the objects that we perceive through our senses are themselves, in fact, *ideas*. That is not to say that what we perceive isn't real. On the contrary, Berkeley's argument is that *reality* is itself composed solely of ideas. Houses, mountains, rocks, and rivers are all ideas. By contrast, Locke and Descartes had both argued that our perceptions were actually the impressions made upon our mind by material objects, which existed independently of our minds. However, Berkeley argued, that assumption could not be sustained by an empiricist philosophy. If we could only have knowledge of what we could perceive, then there was no way to know anything about something that was in principle beyond our perception. Berkeley took Ockham's Razor (the idea that we should not add unnecessary or extraneous ideas to a theory) to Locke's philosophy. Locke's belief in material substance was both unnecessary and extraneous, since Berkeley believed that it was possible to develop a completely cogent form of empiricism while rejecting the concept of material substance. To be, Berkeley argued, is to be perceived (*Esse est Percipi*).

If there is no matter, Berkeley argues, then the world is composed solely of spirits and ideas (by "spirit" Berkeley means

Ideas ~~Matter~~ matter~~s~~.

George Berkeley was ^ here.
perceived to be

an individual active being that is capable of perception). Human beings, as perceiving creatures, are spirits, as presumably are animals and other creatures. Ideas, on the other hand, are objects of perception. The world that we perceive external to our own minds is the world of ideas. While Berkeley denies that the objects of our perception are *material*, he does believe that these objects, these *ideas*, are physical, in the sense that they are composed of tangible objects with which we interact through our senses. Idealism does not mean that we do not experience a sensory world. It simply means that the sensory world that we experience is itself a world of ideas. Thus, while Samuel Johnson may have thought it was a fairly definitive refutation of Berkeley's philosophy to stub his toe on a rock (shouting "I refute it thus!" while doing so), Berkeley himself would have undoubtedly replied that Johnson had missed his point.

If to be is to be perceived, then the logical follow-up question is what happens to objects that *are not* being perceived. In other words, it is not simply a question of whether, when a tree falls in the forest and no one is there to hear if it makes a sound, but rather, if there is no one there, does the tree exist at all? The materialist answer to that question is that objects exist because they depend on some form of material substance independent of perception. But Berkeley argues that objects in the world continue to exist as ideas in the mind of God. God is the immediate cause of all of the ideas that we perceive through our senses and ensures the persistence of sensory objects when there is no one perceiving them. God as an omniscient and omnipresent being is, in essence, always perceiving, and thus ensuring the existence of everything.

But this raises a further difficulty since God's essence is itself something that we cannot perceive. Thus Berkeley seems to have set himself up for the same kind of objection that he lodged against Locke's use of material substance, except with regard to

God. However, Berkeley views God's existence as a necessary inference from his philosophical premises. Because we are not the cause of our own perceptions and cannot choose whether or not to perceive the information of our senses, they must come from another source, that is to say, God. Therefore, even though God is not an object of perception for us, God's existence can be known through the fact that we perceive a world that we recognize as having a source outside of ourselves. Furthermore, because God is the immediate cause of all of our perceptions, God is not, as the deists asserted, a distant clockmaker, but is continually acting in the world as the source of all that is perceptible.

Berkeley's philosophy was an important transition between the relatively conservative empiricism of Locke and the thoroughgoing skepticism of David Hume. But his idealism had an impact far beyond British empiricism. Echoes of his thought can be found in the work of Kant and Hegel, as well as Arthur Schopenhauer and Edmund Husserl. The core question that Berkeley raised—namely, what could be genuinely known by an individual perceiving observer, and how that affects our understanding of the world—continued to resonate throughout modern philosophy. It is also worth noting, in passing, that many of his most significant metaphysical ideas were being developed at almost the same time, and totally independently, by the American theologian and philosopher Jonathan Edwards. There are striking similarities in the arguments that each of them makes both about the nature of the perceptible world and the role of God in creating, preserving, and sustaining that world.

DAVID HUME

The third and in many ways greatest of the British empiricists was David Hume. Born in Edinburgh, he attended the university there at an exceptionally young age and immediately distinguished himself as a scholar. Although his family envisioned a legal career for him, he instead worked as, variously, a tutor, a librarian, a diplomat, and a historian. During his lifetime, he was best known for his *History of England*, but his legacy as a philosopher is rooted in three works: *Treatise of Human Nature*, *An Enquiry Concerning Human Understanding*, and *Dialogues Concerning Natural Religion*. He also made a mark on moral philosophy with his *Enquiry Concerning the Principles of Morals*. Beginning where Locke and Berkeley left off, Hume took their ideas in some radical directions. This thoroughgoing skepticism about metaphysics in general and religion in particular led to accusations of atheism and cost him the prospect of an academic career.

The *Treatise*, his first major work, was not well received; according to Hume, it "fell stillborn from the press." He revised the core arguments of that volume later for his *Enquiry*. Both volumes attempt to press the arguments of empiricism to their logical conclusion. If, as both Locke and Berkeley argued, the only things that we can be said to genuinely know are those things that we obtain directly through our senses, then we are required to abandon not only, as Berkeley argued, the idea of material substance, but also a number of other concepts that seem basic to our understanding of the world, such as cause and effect, free will, and even the very idea of the self. Each of these concepts, which we take to be fundamental to who we are and how we function in the universe, Hume argues, is not rooted in any genuinely observable sense perception.

As with the other empiricist philosophers, Hume argues that we experience ideas as either simple or complex. A complex idea, like "flower," is made up of simple ideas, such as "red." Thus our perception of the world is composed entirely of combinations of ideas, rooted in sense experience. Additionally, we experience what Hume calls "impressions," things like emotions and desires. What we know of the world is the result of our direct sense experience, our memories, and our reflection. However, through our imagination we are capable of constructing ideas about the world that are not themselves rooted directly in any of these things.

For Hume, this tendency to imagine connections where none necessarily exist is at the root of many of our unfounded beliefs about the world. Our belief in cause and effect, for example, arises from the fact that when we see two events happen in constant conjunction with one another, we develop an expectation that they must necessarily do so. But that belief is not rooted in the events themselves, but in our own habits of mind. The fact that it happens regularly is no guarantee that it must happen *necessarily*. It is only

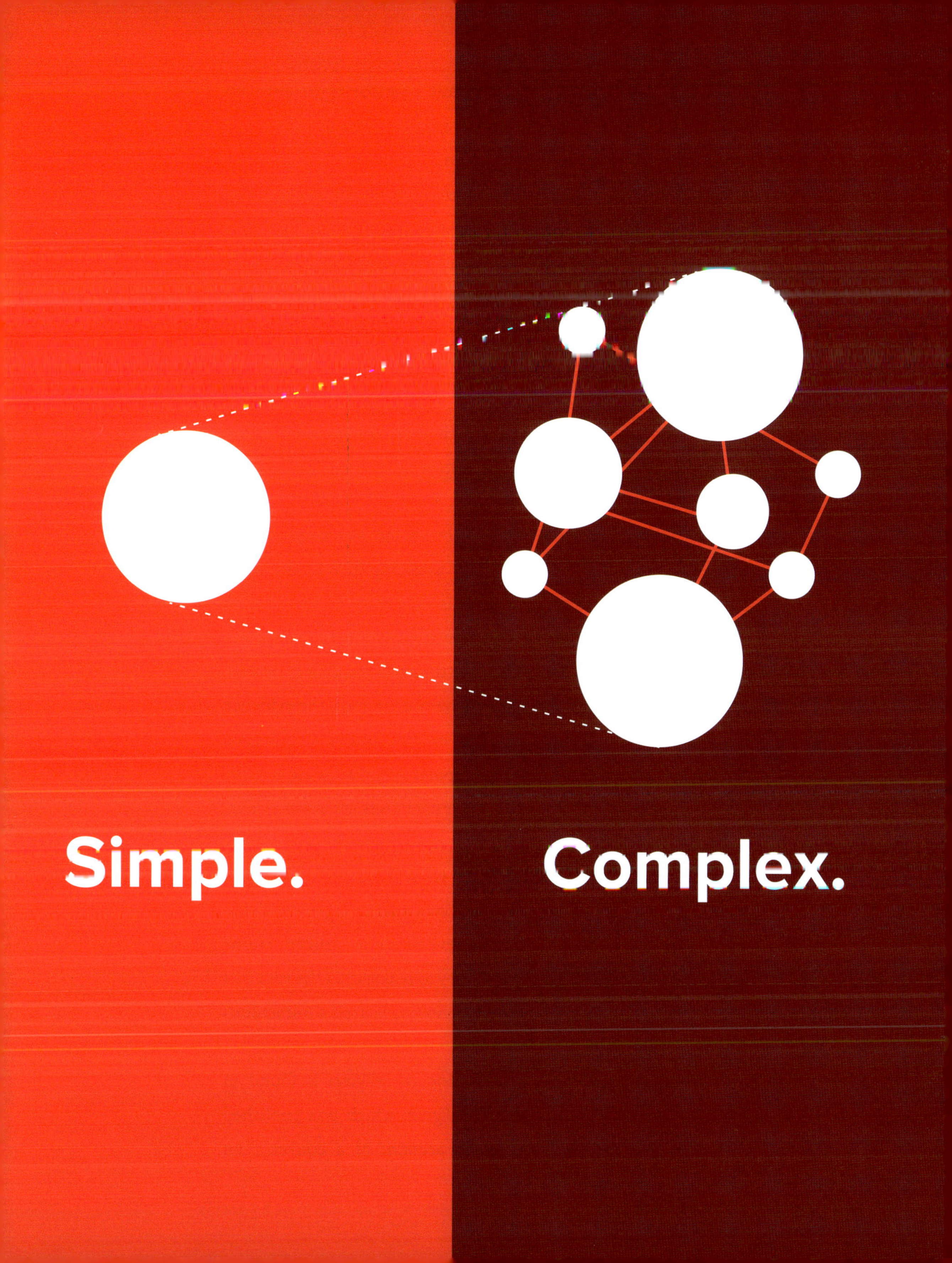
Simple.
Complex.

our disposition to believe so. He makes a similar argument with regard to the idea of the self. We believe that we exist as "selves" not because we observe something that we can call a self. Rather, what we call a self is simply, as Hume argues, a "bundle of perceptions" that we are in the habit of identifying as a continuing thing called a self. By insisting that we cannot claim to know about anything that we cannot directly observe, which cannot be understood to be made up of some combination of simple and complex ideas, Hume is taking the empiricist approach to its natural end. We are only perceptions, sensations, and phenomena. There is no substance, no causation, and no self that underlies the information of our senses. The sense data stand on their own.

Hume's skeptical epistemology was matched by an equally skeptical view of religion. As a historian, he was aware of the problems connected with accurately assessing historical events, and this awareness was reflected in his view of miracles, belief in which he regarded as irrational. Reports of miraculous events, such as Jesus' resurrection, were to be doubted, because they were by definition violations of the laws of nature. As such, the evidence required to believe them had to be extraordinarily convincing. However, as historical documents, reports of miracles are notably flimsy. The authors are unreliable, their narratives are unbelievable, and the events they describe are too incredible. Indeed, there is no human testimony, even the most reliable, Hume argues, that would be compelling enough to convince a rational person that a miracle had taken place. Miraculous events are so unlikely, Hume argues with thick irony, and so contrary to reason that the very fact that people find accounts of them convincing is itself a miraculous event!

Hume's most famous dissection of religion is found in his *Dialogues Concerning Natural Religion*, which was published posthumously. The *Dialogues* is an account of a conversation

The Dialogues
David Hume

between three characters, each of whom defends a particular view of the relationship between God and human reason. The character of Cleanthes argues in favor of the "argument from design," a form of which we encountered in Thomas Aquinas, and which is often found in a modern form in debates surrounding "intelligent design." This approach attempts to demonstrate God's existence based upon the complexity and apparently purposeful nature of the world.

Demea, meanwhile, argues that knowledge of God cannot be inferred from the world itself, but that the only knowledge we can have of God must be purely rational and distinct from human experience. He advocates a form of "cosmological argument," which attempts to demonstrate the existence of God *a priori* as necessary to prevent an infinite causal regression.

The third figure in the debate is Philo, who represents a skeptical perspective. After dispatching Demea's arguments on the grounds that, if true, we can really know nothing whatsoever about God, he then goes on to criticize Cleanthes's arguments. He states that because those arguments depend on analogies between God and the world, their success depends on the strength of the analogies. However, Philo demonstrates that it is impossible to infer an infinite cause from finite effects. Similarly, he argues that the world is no more like a product of human intelligence (such as a house) than it is like an animal or a vegetable. Furthermore, he argues, the existence of evil in the world calls into question the belief in a good creator.

In the end, Philo (who is generally taken to be a mouthpiece for Hume's position) prevails in the argument and, in doing so, has been seen by generations of philosophers to have demolished all of the traditional arguments for God's existence beyond repair. In his wake, it was difficult to uncritically adopt any of these arguments without having to address Hume's objections.

Hume's thoroughgoing skepticism not only brought empiricism to its logical endpoint, but also threw down the gauntlet for any future attempt to create a rational argument for God's existence. It also created the need to think about philosophy in a new way. Neither rationalism nor empiricism had seemed to resolve the underlying metaphysical problems of philosophy, despite their best attempts. It was into these waters that Immanuel Kant waded.

FIVE

KANT

Immanuel Kant's philosophy represented a new departure in philosophy, after the projects of the rationalists and the empiricists seemed to have each produced their own dead-ends. The rationalists' philosophy had led to an apparently endless cycle of metaphysical speculation, in which every philosopher claimed that it was possible through the use of pure reason to know with complete certainty things that were in total contradiction to what other philosophers knew with complete certainty. But if pure reason could not provide knowledge, then reliance on our senses was no better, since it led to utter skepticism. While rationalism built its castles in the air, empiricism salted the earth beneath its feet. In either case, by the end of the eighteenth century, neither appeared to be able to offer a way forward for philosophy.

Enter Kant. Kant was born, raised, and lived his entire life in the Prussian town of Königsberg. His family were German pietists, whose religious faith emphasized a deep personal devotion to God. After his studies, he worked as a tutor for a number of years before eventually returning to teach at the University of Königsberg, where he spent the remainder of his career. Kant was said to be extremely fastidious and disciplined in his personal life, so much so that his neighbors would set their clocks by his afternoon walk.

Kant had been educated in the rationalist tradition of Leibniz, and for the early part of his career he taught and wrote from within that tradition. However, at some point after 1770, an encounter with Hume's philosophy "awoke me from my dogmatic slumber," as he put it. Recognizing the power of Hume's argument but rejecting his conclusions, Kant set about attempting to reconstruct philosophy in such a way as to avoid both the speculative meanderings of the rationalists (whom he referred to as "dogmatists") and the sensory reductionism of the empiricists (whom he called "skeptics"). This led him to a ten-year "silent period" in which he did not write and barely socialized as

So, Kant walks into a bar—
only, he doesn't—for a prerequisite of movement being three-dimensional space, which is merely an illusory construct of pure intuition.

#IJUSTKANTLAUGH

he attempted to solve the puzzle of how to navigate between the Scylla and Charybdis of these philosophical alternatives.

Kant's solution to these problems was most fully articulated in his three "critiques" published between 1787 and 1790. The first of these, the *Critique of Pure Reason*, laid out Kant's approach to metaphysics, while the *Critique of Practical Reason* detailed his approach to morality. The third critique, the *Critique of Judgment*, gave Kant's interpretation of aesthetics. Collectively, these three volumes attempted to reconstruct the basic approach to philosophy that Kant had inherited from his predecessors and create a firmer basis for any future philosophy. (Indeed, Kant titled another of his books *Prolegomena to Any Future Metaphysics*, thereby insisting that anyone who wanted to tackle metaphysics first pass through the gauntlet of his philosophy!)

In the *Critique of Pure Reason*, Kant attempts to grapple with the contradictory answers given by rationalism and empiricism, respectively. Because rationalists seemed to claim we could know too much, while empiricists appeared to end up knowing nothing at all, Kant sought to lay out the parameters by which knowledge of any sort was even possible. Part of the problem, he argued, was that previous philosophers had confused the question of what was *knowable* with the question of what was *believable*. While Hume, for example, ended up concluding that because it was impossible to establish God, the self, and causality by empirical observation, and because they were not self-evident, it was irrational to believe in them. The rationalists, meanwhile, seemed to allow for the rational belief in almost anything. Kant sought to solve this dilemma by, as he put it, limiting reason in order to allow for faith. In other words, by establishing clearly what the limits of reason were, he would also allow for a realm of things in which people could rationally believe but could not prove.

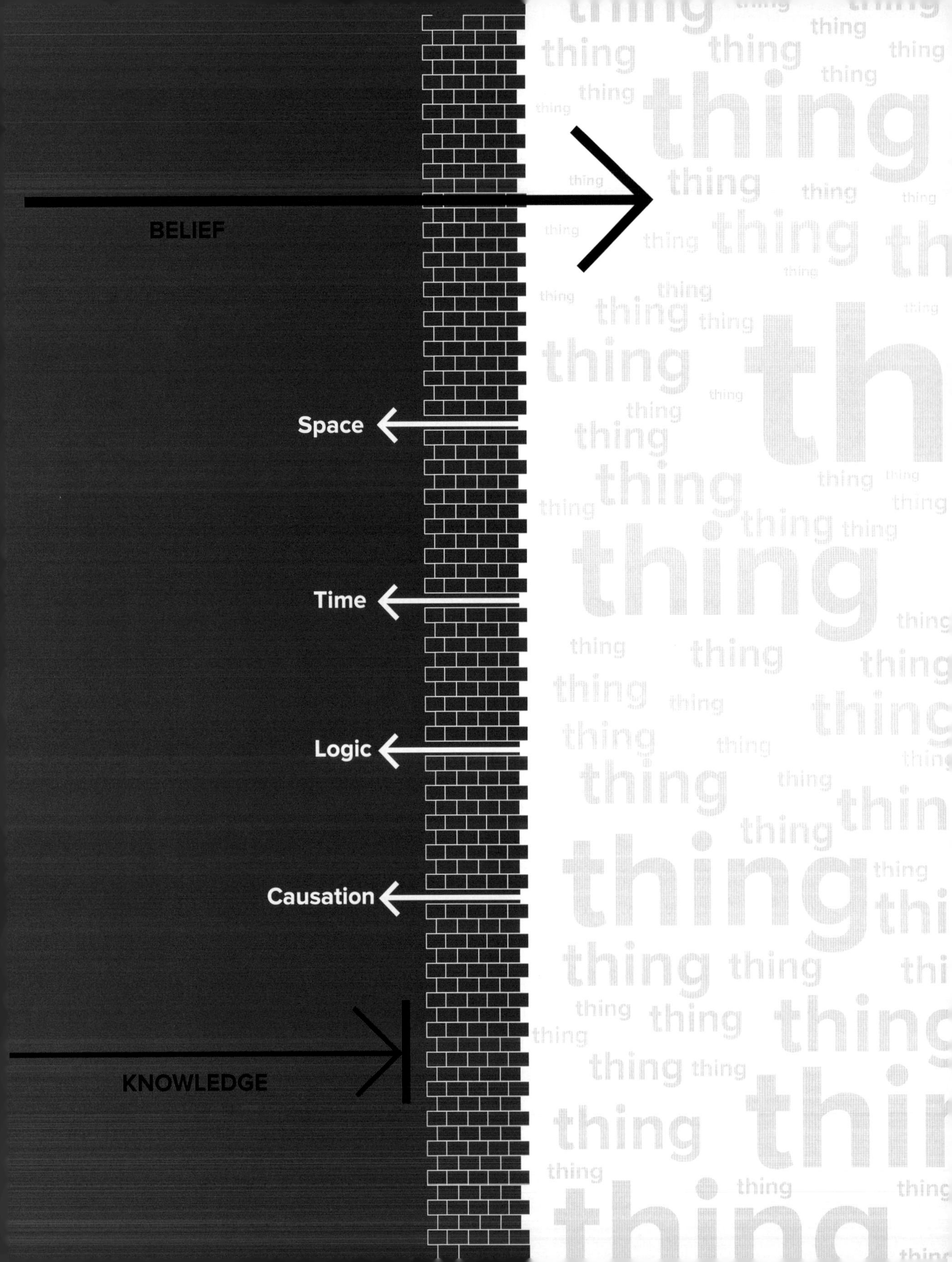
BELIEF
Space
Time
Logic
Causation
KNOWLEDGE
thing

Hume had argued that there were two kinds of propositions, which he termed "analytic" and "synthetic." According to Hume, analytic propositions are *a priori* statements that are self-evident and true by definition, such as mathematical formulas or statements like "all bachelors are unmarried males." Because the definition of bachelor is "an unmarried male," that statement is universally true and can be known without any empirical observation of the world. However, it is also trivial. It does not add anything to our fund of knowledge. Synthetic propositions are *a posteriori* statements that are *not* true by definition but require investigation of the world to determine whether or not they are the case. For example, the truth of statements like "the cat is on the mat" or "the house on the corner is red" cannot be known in advance, but can only be discovered through observation of the actual world. These statements can be true or false, and we learn something about the world through investigating them. According to this approach, all analytic statements are *a priori* and all *a posteriori* statements are synthetic. Hume had argued that any statement that is not either true by definition or capable of being empirically investigated was mere "sophistry and illusion" worthy only of being burned. The problem, however, was that this seemed to eliminate many of the most significant kinds of statements with which philosophy and theology were concerned.

Kant's goal was to retrieve those kinds of statements from Hume's bonfire by asking whether it was possible to have synthetic propositions that were also *a priori*. To do so, he made a distinction between what he calls the phenomenal and the noumenal realms. The phenomenal world is the world of our sensory experience—sight, sound, taste, touch, vision. This is the realm of *a posteriori* empirical propositions. The noumenal world, on the other hand, is the realm of what Kant calls "things in themselves," that is, the reality beyond that which we can perceive with our senses. This realm includes many of the things Hume rejected, such as God, moral law, cause and effect, and the individual self. We can have no direct knowledge of things in themselves, since they are beyond the possibility of sense perception. We can only know what we perceive. We may validly believe things about the noumenal realm (such as that God exists), but we cannot claim to *know* such things. Rather, the world of things-in-themselves is filtered to our consciousness through what Kant calls the "categories of the understanding," a sort of mental filter that enables our minds to make sense of the world. This set of filters contains such things as space, time, logic, and causation. In other words, our minds provide the structure that makes experience possible. We never experience the world itself, only our filtered perception of it.

By doing this, Kant changed the basis on which metaphysics is understood. Previous philosophers had believed that metaphysics was about determining the ultimate structure of the world, whether that was based on our rational analysis of it or our observation of sensory data. Kant said that the world itself is inaccessible to us. We cannot even genuinely *know* the nature of ourselves as we exist in the noumenal world. We can only know that we experience ourselves as individuals in distinction from other individuals. For Kant, metaphysics is about the examination of the human consciousness and its experience of the world.

Kant's approach to metaphysics proved to be highly influential on nineteenth-century philosophy and theology, particularly in Germany. Philosophers such as Friedrich Schelling and Johann Gottlieb Fichte took the basic insights of Kant's philosophy and extended them in new, and often more speculative, directions. Meanwhile, Georg Hegel and Arthur Schopenhauer, each in distinct ways, sought to find a way beyond the wall that Kant had established between the phenomenal and noumenal worlds. Theologians such as Adolf von Harnack and

NOUMENAL
CATEGORIES OF UNDERSTANDING
PHENOMENAL

Friedrich Schleiermacher also each attempted to grapple with the philosophical rules that Kant had laid out in their own reworkings of Christian doctrine.

Kant's moral philosophy was also highly influential. Detailed in the *Critique of Practical Reason* as well as the *Groundwork for the Metaphysics of Morals*, it was based on the premise that morality is ultimately rooted in our rational conception of duty. The only true good, Kant argues, is a good will, that is to say, a will that intends to act in accordance with the commands of reason. But what does reason command us to do? Kant argues that the moral law is encapsulated in what he calls the "Categorical Imperative," that is, the unconditional moral commands of reason. There are, he states, three forms of the Categorical Imperative.

The first form states that we should always act according to rules of action that we can, at the same time, will to be a universal law. So, for example, when confronted with the question of whether we should lie, we can determine the right course of action by asking of ourselves: "What if we created a law that said everyone should lie all the time?" Doing so, he argues, would result in a self-contradiction that would destroy the very act of lying itself, since in a world of universal dishonesty, no one would ever believe anyone. Lying depends on the presumption we have that, most of the time, people tell the truth. In a world where that was not the case, lying would become superfluous. Since we can't consistently make lying into a universal law, he concludes, then we should never do it.

The second form of the Categorical Imperative states that we should always treat other people not as mere means to our own ends but as ends in themselves. That is to say, Kant argues, that other human beings are creatures of reason and dignity. They do not exist for our purposes, but exist for their own sakes. As a result, Kant argues, it is immoral to treat them as instruments for the sake of the fulfillment of our own goals. We can cooperate with others

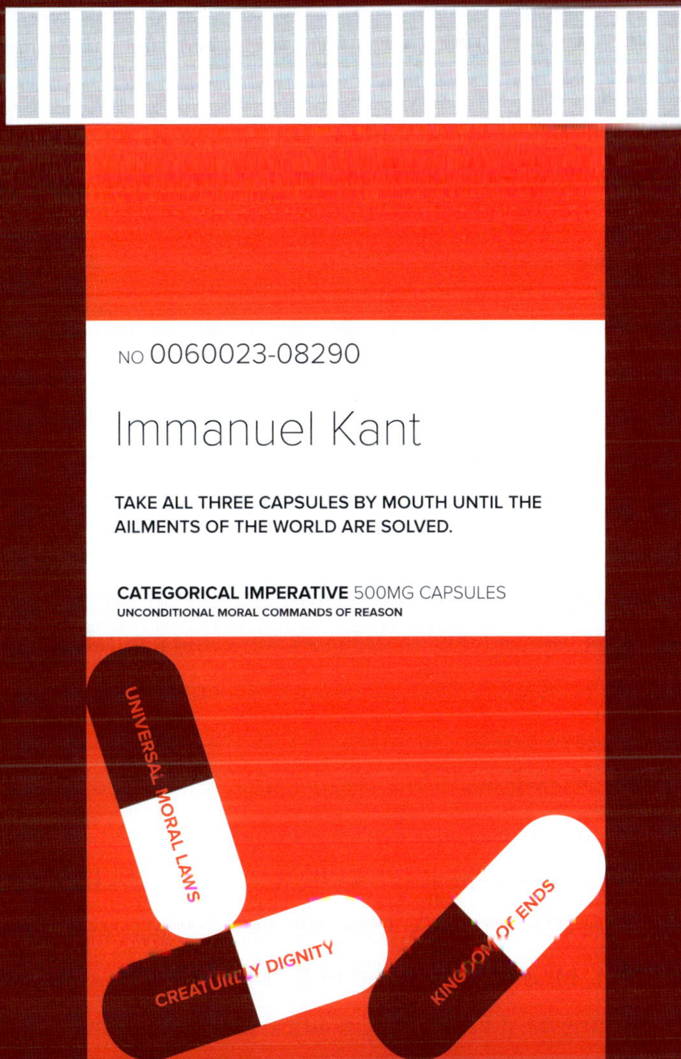
NO 0060023-08290
Immanuel Kant
TAKE ALL THREE CAPSULES BY MOUTH UNTIL THE AILMENTS OF THE WORLD ARE SOLVED.
CATEGORICAL IMPERATIVE 500MG CAPSULES
UNCONDITIONAL MORAL COMMANDS OF REASON
UNIVERSAL MORAL LAWS
CREATURELY DIGNITY
KINGDOM OF ENDS

for mutual benefit, but, he argues, we cannot coerce or manipulate other people, denying them the dignity to which they are entitled as rational creatures.

The third form of the Categorical Imperative states that we should act at all times as though we were members of a kingdom in which the first two principles were consistently followed. Here, Kant's emphasis is on the fact that while we are autonomous moral agents (that is, the moral law is not imposed on us from without, but comes from within us), we live in a society and among other rational creatures, whom we have an obligation to treat at all times as moral agents in their own right. Kant refers to this as a "Kingdom of Ends." He believes that in such a kingdom, each autonomous moral agent would choose those laws that are consistent with the Categorical Imperative, and thus it would be unnecessary to impose the moral law from without. Of course, we do not live in such a society, and so we require external government, but Kant envisions this Kingdom of Ends as an ideal future state, which we should embrace in principle by living as though we were already in it. Kant believed that, in doing so, we would naturally follow the first two principles of the Categorical Imperative.

Kant's moral philosophy, of course, has received a large amount of criticism. Most significantly, it has been argued that since Kant's approach to ethics gives no regard to the *consequences* of our actions, it leads to a morality where principles become more important than outcomes. However, this can lead to moral disaster. Should I, for example, refuse to lie when soldiers appear at my door asking me if I am hiding political dissidents in my basement? To many, it would seem as though Kant must necessarily answer "yes" to that question. However, Kant's philosophy was more sophisticated than that. It would be immoral to lie, but that is not exactly the same thing as being compelled to tell the truth. It may be possible to evade, or even refuse to answer, rather than lie. Lying,

RITUAL
MORALITY

in a sense, is too easy for Kant. It doesn't require us to consider fully the scope of moral options open to us and instead shows us the quick and dirty way out, but it requires us to compromise our own morality in the process. Even so, there are many who find Kant's moral philosophy too pat and dismissive of the ambiguities of moral decision making in a complex world.

Kant also addressed the question of religion in his philosophy, particularly in his book *Religion Within the Limits of Reason Alone* (often translated as *Religion Within the Limits of Bare Reason*). In this book, Kant seeks to separate what he views as essential to religion from the additions of ritual and symbolism that serve to distract from genuine faith. True religion, Kant argues, is fundamentally rooted in morality. As rational creatures, we are capable of developing a good will, but there is within us a natural disposition toward evil. We are nevertheless capable as moral agents of choosing between good and evil. In this way, he attempts to reinterpret the Christian doctrine of original sin. Genuine religion is rooted in virtuous action, not in seeking to curry favor with God through worship and prayer. While God may aid us in our moral lives via grace, God's grace cannot make us good apart from our own free exercise of our will. Jesus Christ, for Kant, functions as a moral exemplar who demonstrates the proper path to morality, though Kant is cagey on the question of Christ's divinity. Religion that focuses on worship, ritual, and the authority of priests and prelates, Kant argues, is not true religion at all, but rather serves as a distraction from the genuine faith that is founded on right moral action. The final hope of true religion is in the ultimate triumph of good over evil and the establishment of a genuine Kingdom of Ends.

Kant's legacy looms large over the history of philosophy and theology. His influence among all of the major philosophers of the nineteenth century, and the way in which that influence

FAITH
REASON

affected how theology has been done ever since, is difficult to overstate. After Kant, one could affirm him, critique him, deny him, or detest him, but one could not avoid him.

SIX

HEGELIAN

GEORG WILHELM FRIEDRICH HEGEL

Georg Wilhelm Friedrich Hegel is the most significant post-Kantian philosopher to emerge from the German enlightenment. His thought set the agenda for European philosophy throughout the nineteenth century and continues to echo in philosophy and theology today. Whereas Kant had sought to end the division between empiricism and rationalism by placing an impenetrable wall between human knowledge and the realm of things-in-themselves, Hegel sought to reconstruct a metaphysical world on the basis of an examination of the development of thought itself. While Kant argued that our understanding of the world was determined and interpreted by the architecture of our minds, Hegel went further, arguing that reality itself is actually the product of mind. However, unlike earlier idealist philosophers, like Spinoza or Berkeley, Hegel does not conceive of mind in the sense of a transcendental metaphysical concept, but rather as a historical process.

Hegel sees history as the outworking of the process by which reason develops itself in the world. By this, he does not mean the way in which human beings become more and more rational creatures (though that is an element). Rather, he views mind, idea, reason, and thought as the structure of reality itself developing over time, and manifesting itself in every dimension of the world, including nature, society, and every dimension of human culture, including art, philosophy, and religion. Furthermore, he identifies the totality of this process with the outworking of God's own being in the world. History begins with God as its starting point, and then culminates in the complete realization of God through the process of philosophical reflection. Religion, in Hegel's thought, is a stage on the way toward that realization of God as what he calls the "Absolute Idea" in history. But it is not the final stage. Rather, religion allows us to access that Absolute Idea of God via images and symbols, whereas philosophy, at its highest level, understands the Idea in a totally abstract form.

In order to see how Hegel reaches this conclusion, it is necessary to trace the development of his argument, which is most fully articulated in his *Phenomenology of Spirit* (which can also be translated as *Phenomenology of Mind*, from the German word *Geist*). Hegel argues that the world is constituted by a conflict between what he calls "moments" and their negations, often referred to as the "thesis" and the "antithesis." Through this conflict there arises a new moment, the negation of the negation, which transcends the original conflict, but which in turn develops a new conflict. This "synthesis" then becomes the new thesis in the process of historical development, producing a new antithesis, and so on. Thus history moves dynamically as the result of the conflict between opposing ideas, producing new ideas at every

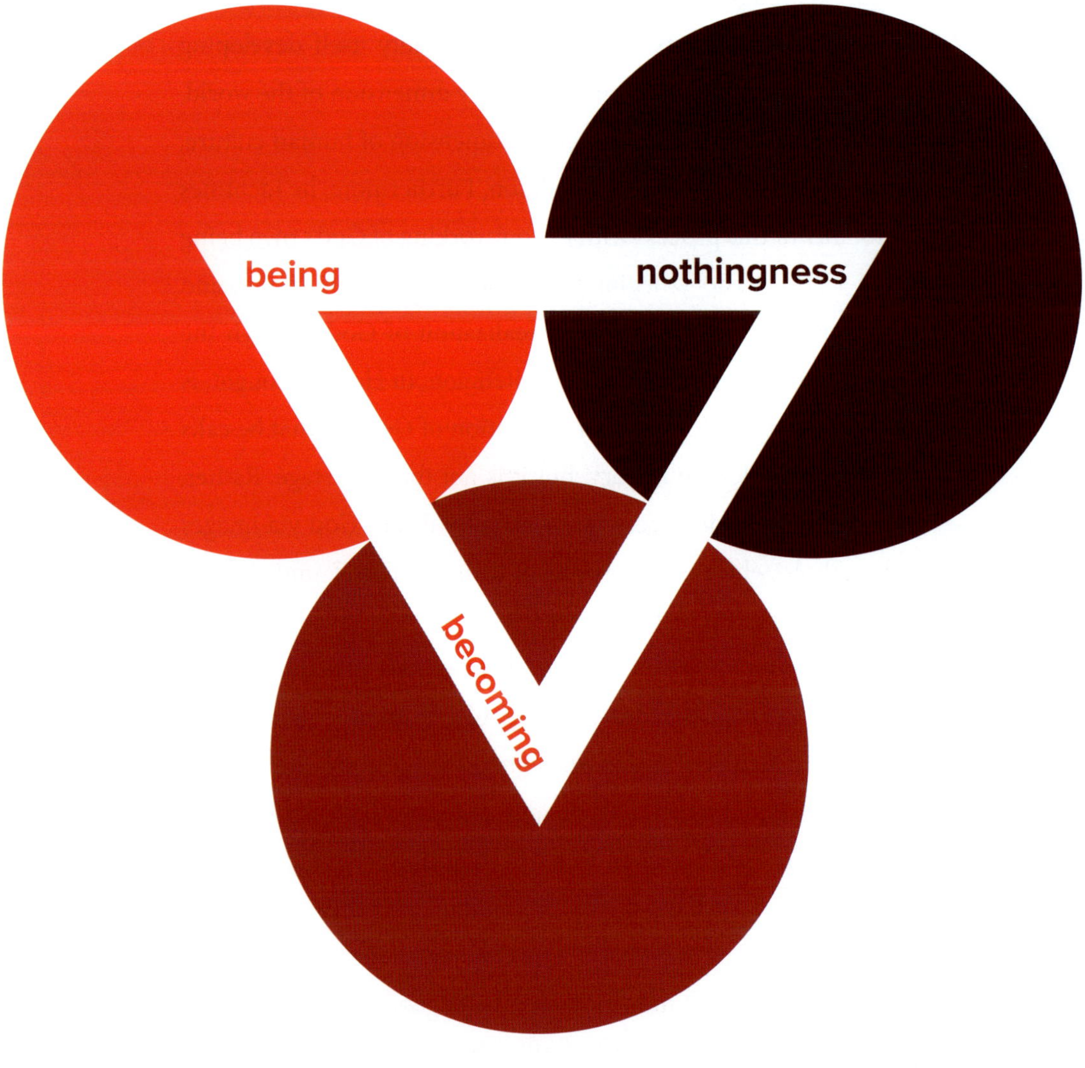
being
nothingness
becoming

BEING
HISTORY
GEIST
BEING

turn, and moving toward a more and more fully developed conception of reality. Once more, it is important to note that for Hegel, this is not just a description of how *human* ideas develop. This is a description of how *reality itself* develops. Hegel refers to this process as the Dialectic.

Hegel begins with the idea of pure Being—Being itself—that in attempting to reflect upon itself produces its opposite, which is to say, Nothingness. This initial metaphysical conflict produces the developmental process of the universe via the process of Becoming. We experience neither being itself nor pure nothingness. The world we inhabit is the world of becoming, the world of phenomena. Everything that happens—every event, every thought, and every sensation—is produced through the process of historical becoming. For Hegel, this is not simply a matter of idle metaphysical speculation. Rather, what he is describing here is the process by which Being itself, which is to say God, undergoes self-alienation, and in the process produces the world. It is, in other words, a doctrine of creation. History is then the process of God's self-rediscovery.

One of Hegel's most famous illustrations of the dialectical process is his account of the relationship between master and slave (usually referred to as the "master-slave dialectic"). This account was deeply influential on some of the more radical members of what came to be known as the "young Hegelians," and particularly on Karl Marx. Hegel attempts to explain the relationship between masters and slaves by taking a page out of Aristotle's *Ethics*. Aristotle had argued that slavery was morally permissible because some people were "naturally" slaves. By this he was referring not to race or ethnicity, but rather to moral character. One who would rather serve than fight is naturally suited to slavery. Hegel adopts this idea but places it in a much more abstract realm. He argues that, in any relation of mind to mind, there is a struggle for power, in which each attempts to dominate the other. That conflict eventually leads to violence, which ends only when the one who is willing to risk his life overcomes the one who values life over liberty. The winner of this conflict becomes the master, and the loser is the slave. The slave gives up his will to his master, acting not on his own behalf, but for his master's sake. However, despite the initial appearance that the slave is subservient to the master, it becomes apparent over time that the master is actually dependent on the slave, since the master becomes incapable of acting on his own behalf and must operate through the slave, who meanwhile through his own action begins to develop a self-consciousness apart from his master and begins to see his own worth reflected in his creative work. Ultimately, the initial appearance of domination and subservience is reversed, as the master becomes enslaved by virtue of his dependency, while the slave overcomes his alienation and achieves self-consciousness through his creative labor. For Hegel, this is not really intended as a political analysis per se. Rather, it is an attempt to show how human self-consciousness develops through the conflict between opposing historical forces and how through the dialectical process each moment of conflict gives rise to a new set of relationships, which itself transforms through further conflict.

Mind, for Hegel, has subjective, objective, and what he calls "absolute" aspects. The subjective conception of mind revolves around the development of human self-consciousness. It is primarily concerned with questions of psychology, the soul, and the nature of conscious thought (i.e., things like memory, intuition, recollection, and imagination). Subjective Mind is concerned with how the intellect develops and becomes self-aware, how it relates to the external world, and how it is capable of feeling, choosing, and seeking after happiness. Subjective Mind is concerned particularly with the internal structure of human thought. For Hegel, this is, again, one moment in the dialectical process.

absolute
mind
objective
subjective

Objective Mind is the response to, or antithesis of, that initial moment of subjective Mind. It is the external realization of subjective thought, and it is experienced in the dynamics of social and political life. Here Hegel deals with questions of morality and social ethics, such as the nature of moral intention and the nature of good and evil. Objective Mind deals with questions of how society is organized, such as law and government. Hegel addresses such questions as the nature of property and contracts, the nature and structure of the family, the organization of civil society, and the characteristics of the constitutional state.

Absolute Mind is for Hegel the highest and most abstract development of the Spirit within history. Absolute Mind is the manifestation of the divine in the context of the historical dialectic. Through this historical process, God is actualized in the world. Through art, absolute spirit manifests itself symbolically as the immediacy of the divine. The inspired artist produces art that seeks to convey a larger truth about the world. In art, God is a unity of nature and spirit, manifested through the artist's work. Various stages of art seek to convey that divine essence in different ways, and Hegel traces the development of the history of art through his dialectical process, finding Romantic art to be the highest stage in this development as art seeks to transcend itself while still remaining art.

In religion, Hegel argues, Absolute Mind manifests itself symbolically through ritual and myth. It exists at a more abstract realm than art, but it is still a form of "picture language" through which we come to understand God on the basis of concrete things, rather than a contemplation of God's being itself. Thus religion strives to overcome the limitations of art, but it does not yet succeed in arriving at the level of pure abstraction found in philosophy, which is for Hegel the highest manifestation of Absolute Mind, through which the process of historical unfolding that originally began with the dialectic of Being and Nothingness finally reaches its goal in the form of absolute knowledge of Being. So God is, for Hegel, ultimately the beginning and end, not only of religion and philosophy, but also the entire unfolding process of history.

Hegel's critics have accused him of being a pantheist, or even of being a covert atheist, ultimately reducing God to the historical process itself. After his death, Hegel's followers divided themselves up into "right wing" and "left wing" factions. The right wing Hegelians attempted to use Hegel's philosophy to reconstruct a conservative form of theological orthodoxy, while the left wing Hegelians (much more successfully) sought to use his thought to push for social and political reforms, and to argue against theological orthodoxy and ultimately on behalf of atheism. The two best known of these "young Hegelians" were Ludwig Feuerbach and Karl Marx.

LUDWIG FEUERBACH

Ludwig Feuerbach's most influential contribution to philosophy was his book *The Essence of Christianity*, in which he took Hegel's idealistic philosophy and turned it on its head. Whereas Hegel argued for idealism, Feuerbach advocated materialism; while Hegel thought the underlying theme of philosophy was religion, Feuerbach believed it was anthropology; and while Hegel believed that the divine was coming to self-realization through the process of human history, Feuerbach believed that God was a projection of human ideals onto an imaginary being. What Hegel had seen as the outworking of the development of mind within the world, Feuerbach saw as the uncovering of an illusion in order to recover what was truly human. Other young Hegelian philosophers, such as David Strauss and Bruno Bauer, covered the same terrain, but Feuerbach offered its most powerful elaboration before Marx.

feuerbach

ILLUSION
PROJECTION
ANTHROPOLOGY
MATERIALISM

hegel

MIND
BECOMING
THEOLOGY
IDEALISM

Feuerbach argued that Christianity, in imagining God according to traditional theistic concepts as an omnipotent, omniscient, and omnibenevolent being stripped from humanity precisely those qualities—power, knowledge, and virtue—that it gave to God. By making God the object into which we pour our own power, knowledge, and goodness, humanity becomes weak, ignorant, and evil. In defining God as perfect, humanity becomes the essence of imperfection. God becomes the sum of all that is worthwhile, and humanity then becomes worthless. Humanity was then placed in the position of needing God to supply those very qualities that it had projected onto God. Divine nature, then, is simply human nature elevated to an infinite degree. In God, we place our essence outside of ourselves as an object of worship and veneration. However, Feuerbach argues, the true task should be to recapture that essence from God and recover it for ourselves. Thus theology, he argues, must be replaced by anthropology. Salvation consists not in seeking a life in God beyond death, but in living fully in this life, having re-appropriated our true nature.

Feuerbach was among the most prominent of a generation of German philosophers who embraced (or were accused of embracing) atheism as their creed. Prior to this, atheism was largely viewed as disreputable at best, and atheists were often considered to be immoral and untrustworthy. Thus the atheism of Feuerbach and the other young Hegelians was considered scandalous. For his part though, Feuerbach argued that the recovery of the anthropological core of religion from theology would allow human beings to become what they were intended to be, as free, moral, and responsible beings in the world. Once God was understood, not as a being apart from us, but our own truest nature, we could strive to embody those virtues we had previously projected onto God within our own lives.

Feuerbach's most significant legacy, however, was in his development of the idea of religion as a form of "projection." This idea would prove to be influential throughout the nineteenth century on philosophers, psychologists, and sociologists from Marx and Freud to Emile Durkheim. However, his ideas were taken furthest by another Hegelian philosopher and social critic, Karl Marx.

KARL MARX

Karl Marx took Feuerbach's materialist transformation of Hegel and further radicalized it, using it as a tool to analyze the way in which economic forces shape human societies. Like Hegel, Marx was interested in the question of how ideas change and develop through history, and like Feuerbach, he rejected Hegel's idealistic vision of the unfolding of Spirit through the historical process. But unlike Feuerbach, he understood materialism not primarily in metaphysical but in economic terms. For Marx, the materials in question were the material conditions through which human beings shaped their lives and social conditions, that is to say land, labor, and capital.

Marx's philosophy was deeply enmeshed with his social activism. As one of the chief theorists of communism in the nineteenth century, philosophy was important to Marx insofar as

“The Opiate for the People”

The foundation of irreligious criticism is: Man makes religion, religion does not make man. Religion is, indeed, the self-consciousness and self-esteem of man who has either not yet won through to himself, or has already lost himself again. But man is no abstract being squatting outside the world. Man is the world of man – state, society. This state and this society produce religion, which is an inverted consciousness of the world, because they are an inverted world. Religion is the general theory of this world, its encyclopaedic compendium, its logic in popular form, its spiritual point d'honneur, its enthusiasm, its moral sanction, its solemn complement, and its universal basis of consolation and justification. It is the fantastic realization of the human essence since the human essence has not acquired any true reality. The struggle against religion is, therefore, indirectly the struggle against that world whose spiritual aroma is religion.

Religious suffering is, at one and the same time, the expression of real suffering and a protest against real suffering. Religion is the sigh of the oppressed creature, the heart of a heartless world, and the soul of soulless conditions. *It is the opium of the people.* (Karl Marx, 1844).

it provided means to aid in the struggle to overcome capitalism and establish European socialism. However, in his early period, he was deeply influenced by Hegel's philosophy and the modifications made to it by young Hegelians like Feuerbach. Ultimately, however, he concluded that philosophy was only useful to the degree that it served as a means for enacting social transformation.

Marx's analysis of historical development was rooted in the way in which economic transformations over time affected the ideological underpinnings of society. Arguing that in each historical epoch, the ideas that tend to predominate favor the interests of whatever class happens to rule, he believed that every dimension of culture is best understood as being, at least in part, a manifestation of economic relations. Thus, while Hegel believed that art, religion, and philosophy could be most fully understood as the highest spiritual achievements of society, Marx believed that they were the super-structure that served to justify and mask the economic power relationships on which they were built.

Marx did not devote a significant portion of his writing to religion. In general, he saw it as simply one aspect of culture among others, all of which were deserving of critique to the degree that they served to sustain the social status quo. There were a number of occasions, however, where he addressed religion directly, most famously in his "Contribution to the Critique of Hegel's *Philosophy of Right*." In this relatively brief treatment, he argues that the criticism of religion (as was done by Feuerbach) could not be separated from the criticism of society as a whole. Religion serves to sustain an unjust status quo by offering it ideological cover, but it has a far more profound role in the life of the believers, offering them the possibility of escape from the suffering caused by injustice and oppression. This is the meaning of his famous dictum that "religion is the opiate of the masses." He does not simply mean that it dulls the senses of the believer, but that it provides them

KARL MARX

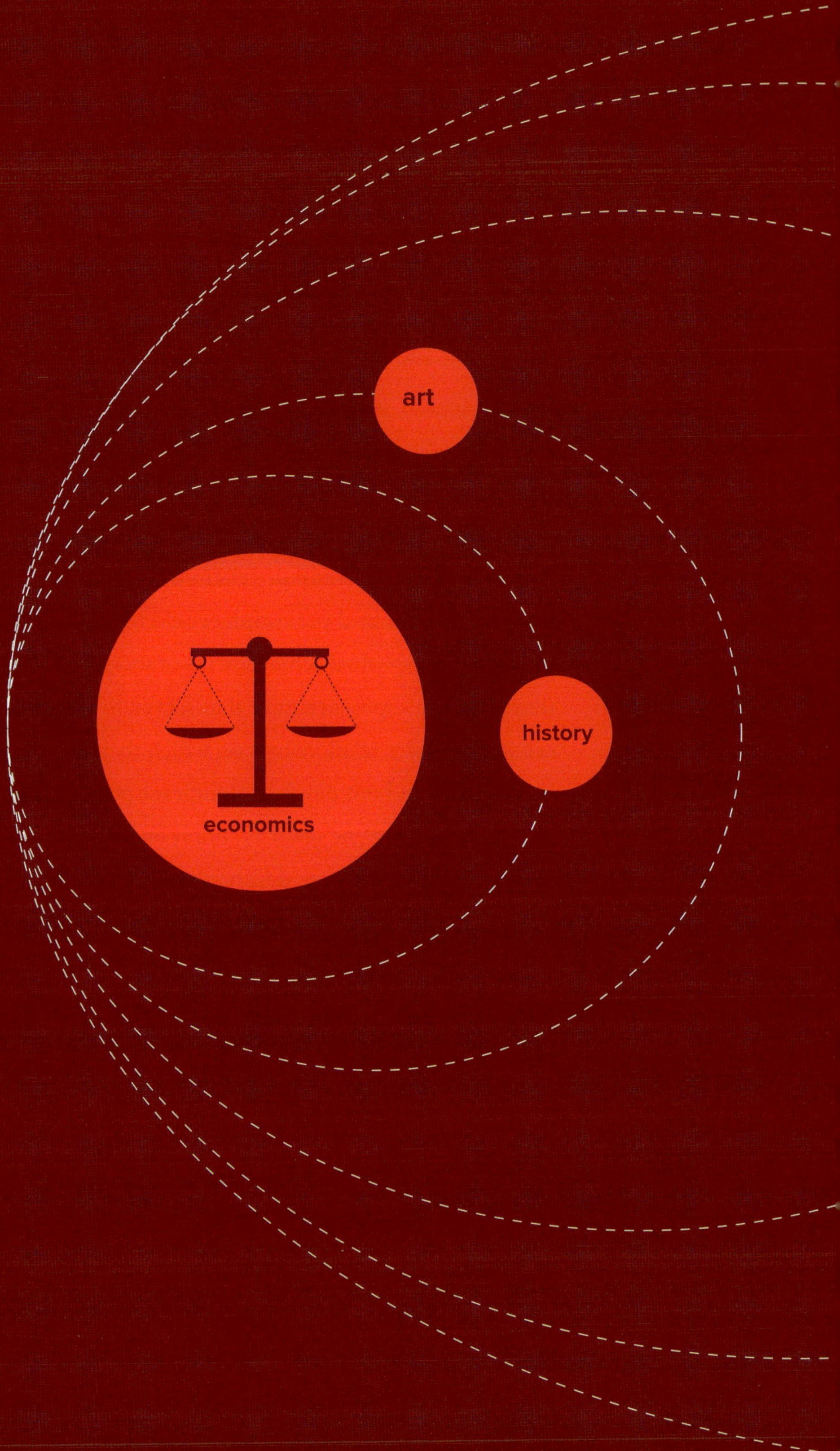

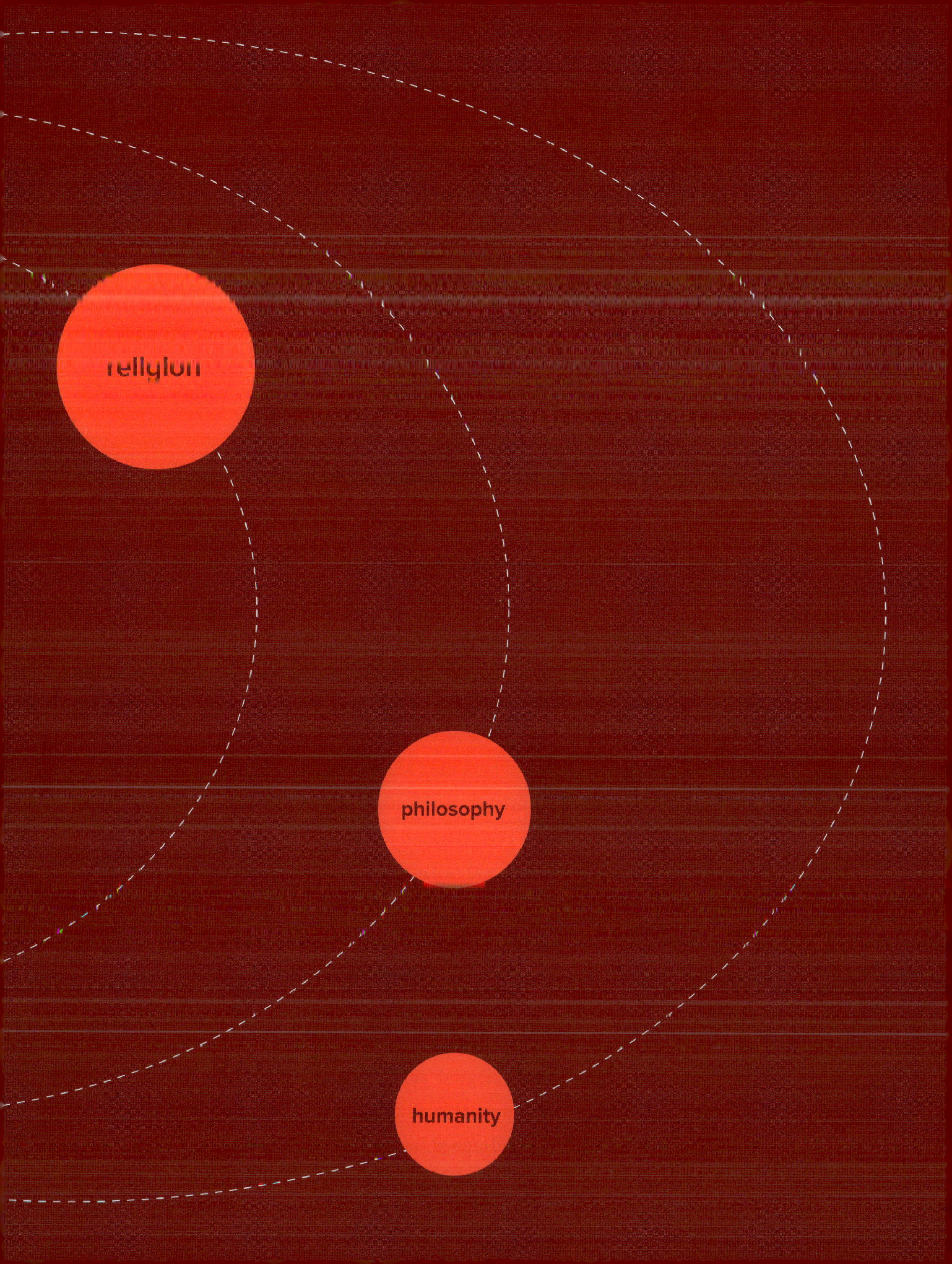
religion
philosophy
humanity

relief from pain. As such, religion provides a genuine benefit to the believer, even if it is not, as Marx believed, true. Criticism such as Feuerbach's, however, seeks to remove the opiate without curing the disease that causes pain. The real purpose of criticism should be to cure the disease of social oppression and class division. Once more, Marx believed that the most significant role that philosophy could play was in making genuine social change possible.

While it is sometimes difficult to separate Marx's critique of religion from the way in which that critique was implemented by many Communist societies, Marx himself does not advocate the abolition or repression of religion. On the contrary, he believes that once the divisions between classes have been overcome and communism has been established, religion will no longer be necessary for human social life, and as such, it will disappear of its own accord. Marx's influence on theology, on the other hand, is seen most clearly in how his economic analysis was appropriated within Christian thought. Both Christian realism in the United States and liberation theology in Latin America were influenced by Marx's description of ideology, power, and class relations. Reinhold Niebuhr's *Moral Man and Immoral Society* and *Reflections on the End of an Era* both used Marx's analysis as a tool for the development of a Christian social ethic, while liberation theologians such as Gustavo Gutiérrez and Jon Sobrino used his approach in the struggle against authoritarian regimes in countries such as Peru and El Salvador.

Ultimately, Hegelian thought in all of its manifestations exercised a strong influence both on Christian theology and on the developing criticism of religion that was coming into its own in the nineteenth century. Hegel was not particularly impressed with his most celebrated theological contemporary, Friedrich Schleiermacher, who had argued that all religion is ultimately rooted not in reason, as Hegel had argued, but in a feeling of absolute dependence. By way of response, Hegel noted that if a feeling of dependence was the key mark of Christian faith, then a dog would make a better Christian than most humans. Nevertheless, Hegel's influence continues to be felt in contemporary theology, particularly in the thought of "theologians of hope" such as Jürgen Moltmann and J. B. Metz, while Marx's critique of economics and ideology can be seen in many forms of liberation thought and Feuerbach's critique of religion as projection serves as the foundation of much contemporary atheism, with which theology has a responsibility to contend within the philosophical and public spheres.

SEVEN

EXIS TENT IALISM

NOTE

While Hegelianism was the predominant post-Kantian philosophy in continental Europe in the nineteenth century, it certainly was not the only one. Perhaps the most potent philosophical (or anti-philosophical) alternative to Hegel was represented by existentialism. Existentialism is less a school of philosophical thought than a particular attitude toward the human condition, reflected in a wide array of diverse thinkers. Unlike most of the other philosophical movements we have analyzed, existentialists do not necessarily share a system of thought as much as they do a mood. Existentialism is interested in the way in which human beings confront what they see as the fundamentally unanswerable dilemmas of existence and the possibility that human life is ultimately a meaningless and absurd farce, to which philosophy can give no final answer.

Existentialism is an unruly philosophical tradition. Many of its leading figures did not "do" philosophy in the ordinary sense of the word, but rather wrote novels, poetry, or collections of aphorisms. Thus Fyodor Dostoevsky, commonly grouped among existentialists, was a novelist, not a philosopher; but his stories, particularly books like *The Underground Man* and *The Brothers Karamazov,* explore themes that are generally associated with existentialism. To the extent that they did write philosophical treatises, it was not always clear how they intended those treatises to be read. This was nowhere more evident than in one of the key figures of existentialism, Søren Kierkegaard.

SØREN KIERKEGAARD

Søren Kierkegaard is the best-known representative of that unruly and difficult-to-categorize character of existentialist philosophy. While he was chiefly concerned with the question of how one could strive to be Christian within a society that was already self-consciously Christian, it could be difficult to actually discern what he believed, in part because he often wrote pseudonymously, picking fights under assumed names, not only with other writers with whom he disagreed, but often with *his own other pseudonyms*. This literary strategy allowed him to explore the problems of faith, aesthetics, and morality from a variety of angles by pitting his various assumed identities against one another, but it also makes determining the views of the "real" Kierkegaard exceptionally difficult. Nevertheless, there were several themes that he addressed across his various pen names, and several of his works stand out as being particularly important in the subsequent development of existentialist philosophy.

A central problem for Kierkegaard had to do with what it meant to take a stand as an individual in a society that demanded conformity. In the context of Denmark in the nineteenth century, this had to do particularly with what it meant to be Christian. If Christian faith was simply conformity with the given religious prejudices of society, then individual Christian virtue was no great accomplishment, nor did it reflect the life and teaching of Jesus Christ. If there is nothing exceptional about Christian faith, it is not worth very much. Faith, then, must mean standing apart from the status quo and against conformity with social norms and expectations. Kierkegaard's own life reflected some of that unconventional spirit. He loved, proposed to, and ultimately broke off his engagement with a woman named Regina Olsen. His reasons for ending the relationship were never clear, but it remained an element of his writing throughout his career. He also opened himself up to public ridicule by picking a fight with a well-known satirical magazine, which then proceeded to mock and caricature him mercilessly.

Philosophically, his individualism was represented by resistance to the predominance of Hegelian philosophy. Hegel's system, he argued, could account for every dimension of human existence, and yet in doing so it consumed all individual identity and choice within the larger framework of the dialectic. The only way for an individual to assert his or her identity in light of that framework was through a wholesale rejection of it.

In *Either/Or*, widely considered to be Kierkegaard's *magnum opus*, he considers two primary orientations toward life. Utilizing the pseudonym of "Victor Eremita," Kierkegaard presents these two orientations as an exchange of letters between two other characters. The first volume purports to be a collection of papers gathered by "A," an aesthete (another one of Kierkegaard's many pseudonyms). A is concerned with sensuality and self-interest. The

One must go further; one must go further.

Søren Kierkegaard, *Fear and Trembling*

highest expression of the aesthetic stage is found in the experience of love's first flush, when it is at its most intense. He represents this through passages from the diary of "Johannes the Seducer" (a pseudonym), whose life is dedicated to the avoidance of boredom, but who is more interested in exploring the possibility of seduction than in actually doing it. Ultimately, however, the aesthetic stage is unsatisfying, leading only to despair (which Kierkegaard names as the "sickness unto death"). This leads him to the second, ethical stage.

This second stage is represented by the character of "Judge Vilhelm" (yet another pseudonym), who argues with A over the value of the moral life in opposition to a life of sensual pleasure. Judge Vilhelm's perspective is heavily informed by Kantian philosophy, and he argues against A's concern with the immediacy of experience in favor of the moral life. Aesthetic existence is passive, whereas ethical life is oriented toward active engagement with existence. Morality does not deprive life of aesthetic value, he argues, but deepens it. He urges A to consider the benefits of marriage and to seek a balance between the ethical and aesthetic approaches to life. At the same time, however, the Judge cannot help but note that, in the end, even the highest achievements of human morality fail to live up to what is demanded of us by God, before whom we are always in the wrong. Ultimately, neither aesthetic existence nor ethical life can provide a final answer to the fundamental problem of human existence. For that a third, religious stage is necessary.

In one of his most widely read works, *Fear and Trembling*, Kierkegaard examines this third stage through the biblical story of Abraham. When God commands Abraham to sacrifice Isaac, it places the patriarch in an impossible situation. There is no external reference point from which Abraham can decide what to do—no law, no morality, no code can tell him, with certainty, whether this is God, and even if it is, what his response should be. Abraham is forced into the position of having to *choose*, in the absence of certainty, what to do, and to bear the responsibility for his choice. Thus he is at once radically free in the face of God's command and yet inescapably responsible for it as well. He could choose to reject God or to deny that it is even God giving the command. The situation, says Kierkegaard, requires Abraham to make a leap of faith, to trust in a God about whom he has no certainty, and from whom he can demand no guarantees. Abraham is required to act, required to obey God, but lacks any moral reference point from which to do so. Thus, Abraham engages in a "teleological suspension of the ethical"—forgoing morality out of obligation to faith in God. As a result, Kierkegaard argues, Abraham represents the ideal "knight of faith."

The core themes of Kierkegaard's writing—individualism, subjectivity, freedom, responsibility, and faith—became core concepts with which later existentialists engaged in varying ways. Kierkegaard's thought wielded tremendous influence on twentieth-century theology and can be detected in the work of thinkers from Karl Barth to Paul Tillich to Emil Brunner and Reinhold Niebuhr. At the same time, the *mood* of this writing, his concern with dread, anxiety, despair, doubt, and death, permeated much of twentieth-century philosophy and literature. Existentialism divided into two camps. Christian existentialists, such as Karl Jaspers, continued to see value in Kierkegaard's analysis of individual responsibility in the presence of God. Atheist existentialists, however, began from much the same starting point as Kierkegaard, but contemplated what the ideas of individualism, freedom, and responsibility looked like within the framework of a godless universe. Two of the most prominent and influential of these atheist existentialists were Friedrich Nietzsche and Jean-Paul Sartre.

FRIEDRICH NIETZSCHE

One consistent theme among existentialist philosophers is their idiosyncratic approaches to their own lives. They embodied the existentialist commitment to individual self-realization in their own choices. This was nowhere clearer than in the life and work of Friedrich Nietzsche. Born to a pious Christian family, he rebelled early against the strict Christianity of his mother and sister. Abandoning their ambitions for him to become a pastor, Nietzsche went on to study linguistics and philology. He gave up a promising academic career at a young age, largely due to his frail health, and lived as a sort of literary vagabond until he suffered a mental collapse in 1889. Sadly, in the years after he was no longer capable of caring for himself, his sister appropriated both his name and his literary legacy in order to promote her dedication to German nationalism and anti-Semitism, sentiments that Nietzsche himself found repugnant.

Much like Kierkegaard, Nietzsche delighted in the use of irony, hyperbole, and misdirection in his writing. He was a master of the barbed aphorism, but his wit sometimes concealed a very profound philosophical analysis. At its core, Nietzsche's philosophical objective was to tear down the edifice of Western philosophy, religion, and morality in order to clear the path for the rise of a new way of being in the world. While Nietzsche's writing covered a great deal of ground, there are several central themes to which he returned again and again.

The first of those ideas is the Will-to-Power. Nietzsche was scornful of traditional conceptions of morality, arguing that they were expressions of a form of herd-mentality. Any ethic that placed the well-being of others at its core was simply an expression of an internalized slave morality. And, he continued, that is precisely what most people are—slaves, suited only for serving others. However, the genuinely great human being transcends that morality through the Will-to-Power, the creative principle through which individuals re-create the world to suit themselves and their desires. The ultimate expression of the Will-to-Power is embodied in what Nietzsche called the "Overman." The Overman acts wholly out of his sense of self-determination and for his own sake, dominating others and fashioning existence in whatever manner pleases him. While slave morality embodies principles of love, self-giving, pity, and sacrifice, the morality of the Overman embraces cruelty, passion, domination, and mastery. Nietzsche's attitude is elitist and aristocratic. He was scornful of most ordinary human pursuits, contemptuous of democracy, and dismissive of popular culture. This is philosophically expressed through this tension between the Overman on the one hand and the herd on the other.

Nietzsche argues that his approach to morality is not nihilistic, but rather embraces the true spirit of human life—self-creation and overcoming. It is traditional morality, Christian morality, which is ultimately nihilistic in that it encourages self-destruction and ultimately death. The Will-to-Power, argues Nietzsche, is an ethic that embraces life in all of its fullness, and as such must be inveterately opposed to Christianity's ethic of self-abnegation. The real distinction in morality is not between good and evil, but between good and bad. Christianity calls evil those things that contribute to individual self-fulfillment and good those things that encourage slave morality. Nietzsche's ethic embraces self-fulfillment and nobility of spirit as genuinely good, abandons the category of evil as being merely a way of delegitimizing authentic human excellence, and identifies the slave morality of Christianity as being an expression of a base spirit, as being bad, unworthy, and contemptible.

Another central theme in Nietzsche's philosophy is the Death of God. He first addresses this idea in *The Gay Science*, in which he tells a parable about a madman running through the streets proclaiming God's death. When he is mocked by the complacent townspeople, who ask who it is that has killed God, he cries out that we have killed him and now have to live with the consequences of God's death, an act for which no atonement or repentance is great enough.

Far from being a celebration of atheism, this proclamation of God's death is filled with dread for its implications. By proclaiming not merely that God does not exist but that God has in fact been killed, Nietzsche is calling into question the kind of complacent atheism represented by the townspeople. God's nonexistence is a philosophical problem, but God's death is also a tragedy—one that requires a complete reevaluation of all of our prior assumptions about the world, our place in it, and the meaning and purpose of human life. To proclaim that God is dead, for Nietzsche, means that the whole foundation of human existence and the moral structure of Western society has been shaken and that all objective reference points for human life have been destroyed along with God.

GOTT IST TODT. UND WIR HABEN IHN GETÖDTET!

GOD IS DEAD. AND WE HAVE KILLED HIM!

nietzsche

A third motif that is central to Nietzsche's philosophy is the idea of "eternal recurrence," that everything in the world repeats itself again and again with absolutely no change or variation. Nietzsche proposes this not as an actual metaphysical account of the world, but rather as a way of expressing the fundamental human condition. He asks his readers to imagine being approached by a demon who tells them that they must live every moment of their life again and again, exactly as they have, an infinite number of times. How, he asks, would his readers receive such news? Would they fall to the ground in despair to contemplate living an identical life without variation over and over again, or would they embrace the demon as a savior? Nietzsche's moral point is implied: If you would not want to live your life over and over again the same way infinitely, with no change, why would you want to live it that way even once?

Nietzsche's influence on twentieth-century philosophy was enormous. He is *the* major dialogue partner, along with Hegel, of almost all continental European philosophy, from Martin Heidegger and Edmund Husserl to Albert Camus and Michel Foucault; his ideas have loomed over all subsequent philosophical inquiry. In theology, his work was less pronounced but no less present. The great theologians of the twentieth century all engaged with him on some level, and in the wake of World War II, the idea of the Death of God became increasingly credible as a theological stance, even leading to the emergence of a short-lived "death of God theology" in the early 1960s. While Christian existentialism is to a large extent rooted in Kierkegaard's writing, atheist existentialism takes its cues from Nietzsche, although Nietzsche never used that term to describe his thought. Many thinkers sought to articulate the idea of existentialism as a particular and coherent philosophical movement but few articulated it as succinctly as Jean-Paul Sartre and Simone de Beauvoir.

Eternal Recurrence

JEAN-PAUL SARTRE & SIMONE DE BEAUVOIR

Twentieth-century existentialism emerged as a movement in the 1930s and reached its apex of popularity in the years after World War II. As was typical of the previous century's existentialist movement, it was diverse and hard to pin down. Borrowing from philosophies as varied as Marxism and phenomenology—as well as utilizing the insights of Kierkegaard, Nietzsche, and other earlier figures—existentialism in its modern form crossed philosophical, political, and literary boundaries in seeking to define the human condition in what was sometimes called the "Age of Anxiety." While it would be difficult to select any one figure as being exemplary of the movement, it was given one of its clearest treatments by the French philosophers Jean-Paul Sartre and Simone de Beauvoir.

Sartre's writing covered a variety of genres, from novels and journalism to biography and philosophical treatises. As a thinker, he covered material as diverse as the phenomenology of Emund Husserl to the novels of Gustav Flaubert. Politically radical, he was associated with the Communist Party in France and was an active member of the French Resistance during World War II. His writing had a deep influence on the post-war intellectual climate, particularly his emphasis on individual responsibility in the face of the moral ambiguity of the age.

Sartre's early writing is exemplified in his novel *Nausea*, which depicts the existential crisis of a man seeking to find meaning in an absurd and meaningless world. At one point, the protagonist finds himself staring at a tree, unable to recognize it for what it is once he has let go of his prefabricated framework for comprehending it. It becomes for him simply an undifferentiated, horrifying mass. In the absence of any prepackaged system of meaning, in a universe without God, all of existence potentially takes on this meaningless, undefined character. It is finally, he argues, we who make our own meaning by establishing our own basis for existence, rather than placing that responsibility on someone or something else. He explores this theme in depth in his later work *Being and Nothingness*.

One problem for Sartre is the reality of the existence of other people. Just as Sartre's protagonist in *Nausea* makes the tree an object of his gaze—and by doing so transforms it into a thing—so we are constantly subject to the gaze of other human beings, who inevitably try to make us things in their turn. Here we see an updated version of Hegel's master-slave dialectic, processed through Husserl's phenomenology, whereby simply in the encounter with other individuals, we find ourselves in a battle for dominance: Who will be the thing, the object of the other's gaze? Sartre dramatizes this problem in his play *No Exit*. In the play, three characters find themselves in hell, each called on to be the tormentor of the other two. The vicious circle of domination

Hell is other people.

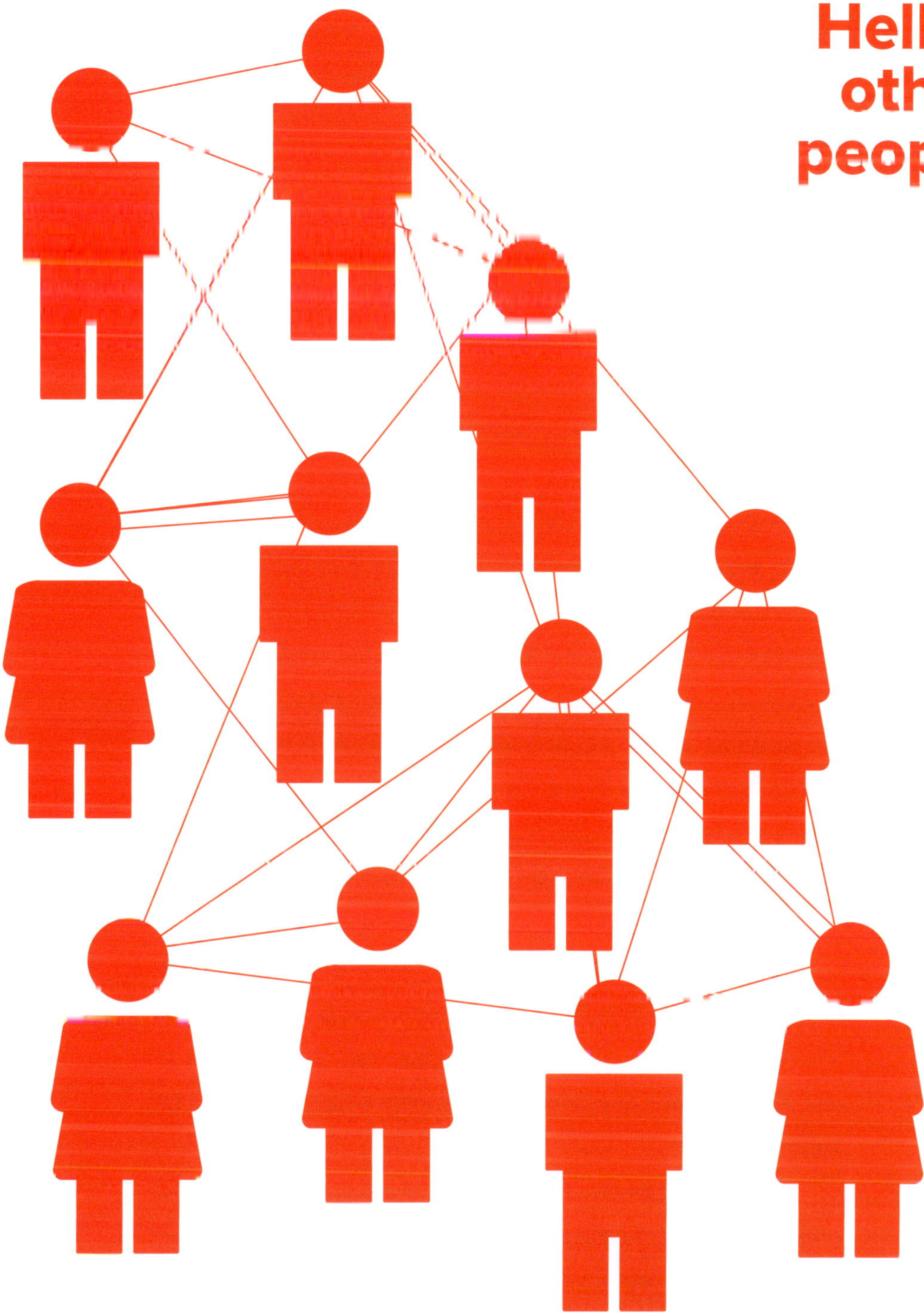

and victimization that occurs in the room from which they cannot (or rather will not) escape becomes their own self-created hell, which in the end they each freely choose to inflict upon the others because, as one character declares, "Hell is other people!"

Sartre's most succinct description of existentialism as a philosophy is found in his essay "Existentialism is a Humanism." In this short piece, he explains that atheistic existentialism, which is the position he advocates, operates from the premise that existence precedes essence. That is to say, there is no pre-given human nature that defines who we are or how we should be in the world. Rather, as human beings, we find ourselves in the world, and it is up to us to make our own meaning out of our experiences and decisions. Because there is no cosmic reference point outside of ourselves, we as individuals are wholly responsible for our actions and there is no standpoint from which to determine that any one course of action is objectively better than any other. This condition, he argues, leads the existentialist to experience life as a matter of anxiety, forlornness, and despair. Ultimately, the only standard that we can use to evaluate our actions is whether they are free, authentic, and a reflection of our own self-determination. When we act in good faith, true to our own self-definition, then we are acting in a worthwhile manner, whereas when we seek to shunt off our responsibility onto other people or circumstances, we are exercising bad faith. Ultimately, Sartre argues, the question of God's existence or nonexistence is rather beside the point, since whether or not God exists, as Kierkegaard had observed in *Fear and Trembling*, the question of human responsibility remains the same.

Simone de Beauvoir was Sartre's long-time collaborator and companion. Her contributions to philosophy extended beyond her existentialist work to her substantial writing on feminism. Like Sartre, she led an unconventional life and strongly influenced the thought of her contemporaries. Among her many significant works, the one that most fully exemplifies the existentialist ethos is *The Ethics of Ambiguity*. In this book, she lays out a moral theory rooted in existentialist thought. She argues, with the other existentialists, that the human condition is fundamentally one of freedom, with no external basis and no pre-given direction. However, true freedom is not merely individualistic, but rather expresses itself through concern with and in relation to other human beings. This relational dimension of de Beauvoir's thought distinguished it from the moral pessimism of Sartre's viewpoint and also connected it to her feminist writing.

Her most acclaimed work in feminist thought is *The Second Sex*, an analysis of the way in which women are socially defined to conform to particular roles. If, as Sartre had argued, "existence precedes essence," then there is no pre-given definition of what it means to be a woman. Men have defined womanhood in terms of their Otherness, cloaking them in an aura of mystery, but only through engaging in a process of self-definition can women find authentic freedom for themselves apart from the roles defined for them by men. Doing so is a necessary condition for overcoming patriarchal structures that contribute to women's oppression.

Existentialism's influence began to decline in the 1960s but remains an important element of nineteenth- and twentieth-century philosophy. Other streams of philosophical thought have adopted and adapted Nietzsche's contributions, in particular certain brands of postmodernism and post-structuralism. Perhaps his most lasting contribution to theological discourse has been in his role as chief opponent and villain in much twentieth-century Christian literature, though in the past decade, his significance for theology as a thinker has been increasingly recognized. Meanwhile, Kierkegaard was deeply influential on the development of twentieth-century theology, particularly on figures such as Paul

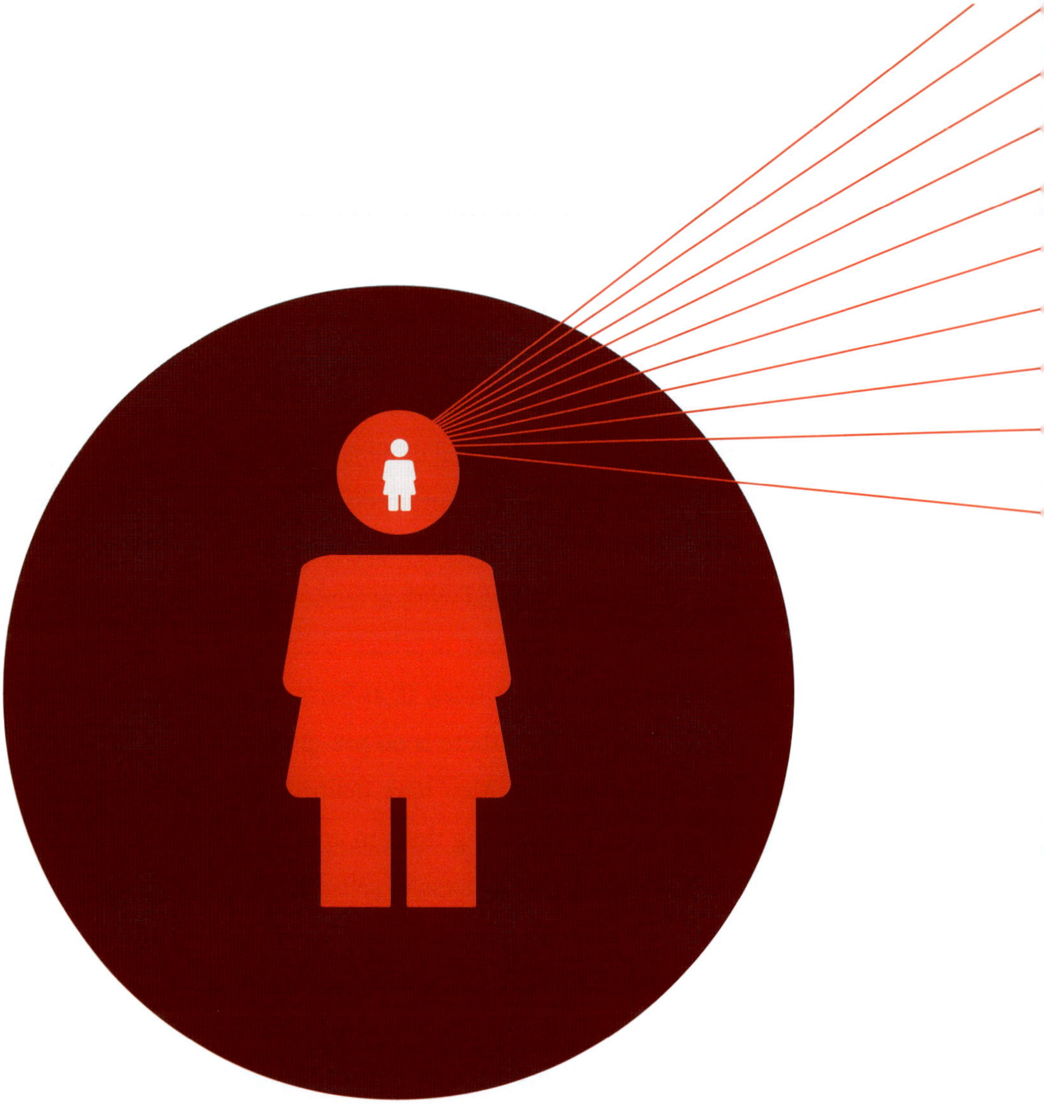

One is not born, but becomes a woman.

Simone de Beauvoir, *The Second Sex*

Tillich, Karl Barth, Emil Brunner, and Reinhold Niebuhr. The existentialism of Sartre and de Beauvoir affected the generational outlook of those theologians who studied in the 1940s through the 1960s, although their particular contributions to theology were more diffuse. Nevertheless, both postmodern and feminist theologies as we know them today owe an immense amount to their work.

EIGHT

CON TEMP ORARY

NOTE

In this final section, we focus on some of the philosophical trends that have had the most influence on theology over the past thirty years. While there are a number of avenues of inquiry we could explore, we are going to focus on four of the movements that have had the most pronounced impact on how contemporary theology is done: process thought, linguistic philosophy, postmodernism, and feminist philosophies. To some degree, each of these approaches is informed by the others, and the boundaries among them are not always clear. However, we will attempt to touch on some of the key figures and themes within each and what makes each distinctive in its own right.

PROCESS THOUGHT

Process thought has a lengthy pedigree, which arguably extends back to ancient Greek metaphysical concepts, and which echoes in many ways the ideas of historical movement that are central to Hegel's philosophy. It is, however, a distinct philosophical movement, one that emerged within twentieth-century Anglo-American philosophy as a way of accounting for the nature of reality in terms of movement, evolution, and development, rather than static conceptions of Being. It differs from Hegel's thought primarily because it does not rely on the dialectical structure through which Hegel views history as moving, but rather depends on the idea of entities in the world as being not "things," but "occasions," possibilities of experience existing within particular objects or creatures.

PROCESS THOUGHT

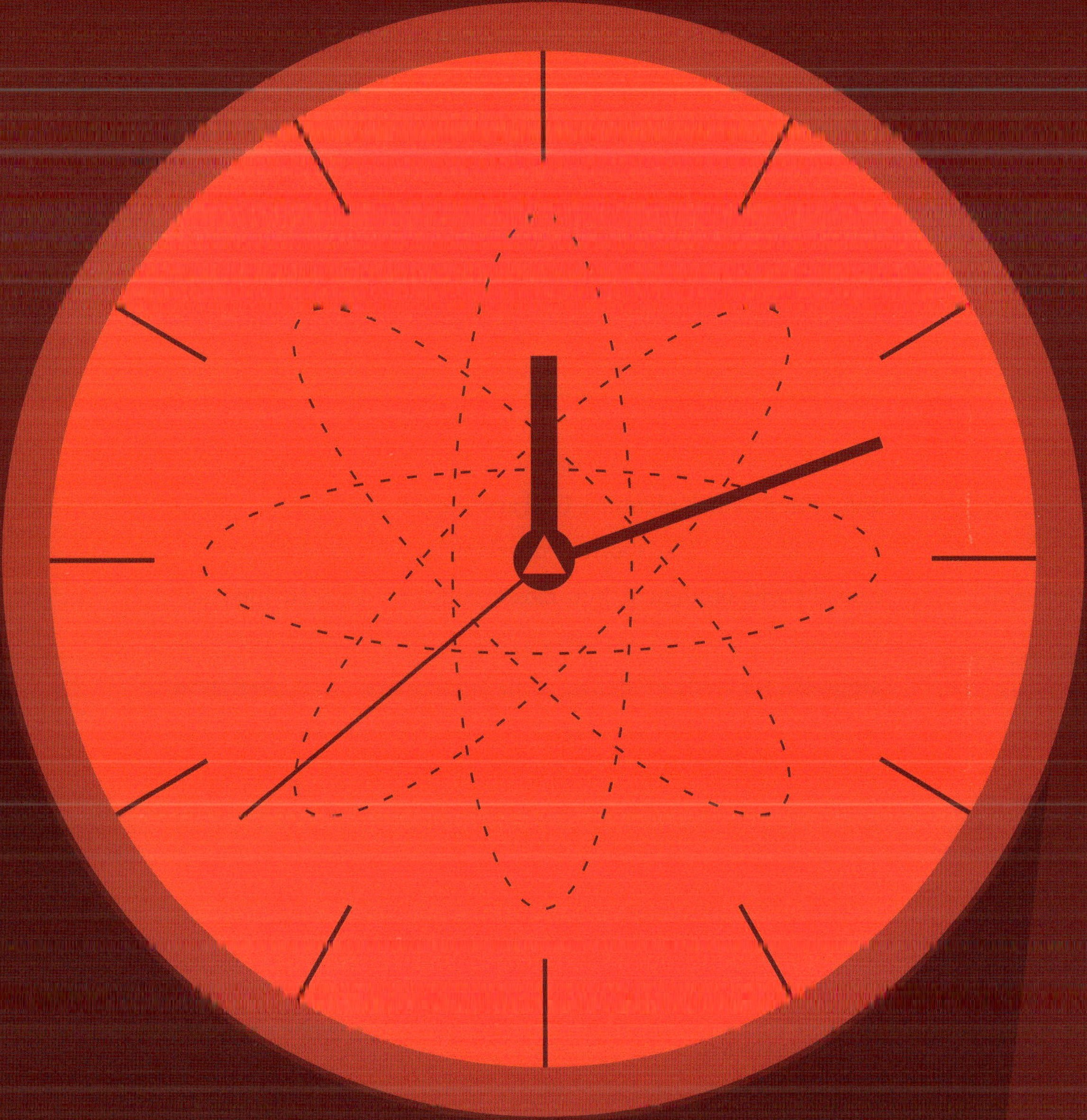

Alfred North Whitehead, an American philosopher who had worked extensively in the field of logic, made the first major contribution to the field of process thought with his book *Process and Reality*. In this book, he argues that there is a distinction between what he calls "actual entities" and "abstractions." Actual entities are existing things that are replete with creative possibility and that exist in a state of *becoming*, continually realizing and giving rise to new possibilities. Abstractions, on the other hand, are possible entities that do not themselves exist. God, for Whitehead, exists within every actual entity, both within and beyond time. God thus embodies all possible experience but is not bound by it. Whitehead thus affirms what has become known as a panentheistic understanding of God, which sees God as in everything that exists but not limited by existence (as opposed to a pantheistic conception, which identifies God and the existing world).

Charles Hartshorne developed Whitehead's process thought and brought it into closer conversation with theology. In *Anselm's Discovery*, he offers a defense of Anselm's ontological argument for God's existence, while arguing that God's perfection is not static, but rather undergoes development toward greater and greater realization. Like Whitehead, his conception of God is panentheistic, viewing God as being both within and beyond all things.

Process thought has had a strong influence on much recent theology. Picking up on Whitehead and Hartshorne, process theologians have sought to apply the metaphysical assumptions of their thought to Christian doctrine generally, as well as applying it to questions of morality and politics. In its emphasis on continuity in the God-world relationship, and God's immanence in creation, it has proven particularly influential in the development of some streams of ecologically oriented theology.

LINGUISTIC PHILOSOPHY

Modern philosophy was often said to be characterized by its "subjective turn," that is, with Descartes, philosophy began to concern itself more and more with the character of the knowing subject. In the twentieth century, philosophy has been said to have taken a "linguistic turn," a turn to a consideration of the way in which our reality, in all of its dimensions, is not only interpreted, but even constructed, on the basis of the language we use to describe it. Emerging from the Anglo-American analytic approach to philosophy, its roots lie in the empiricist approach of Locke, Berkeley, and Hume, though many of its most prominent proponents were German or Austrian.

Early linguistic philosophers, such as Gottlob Frege, began by investigating the structure of language and the difference between the terms we use to describe things and the things to

Language disguises thought.

Ludwig Wittgenstein

which they referred. Using mathematics as a model, he sought to break the structure of language down to its most basic logical components. This idea was later taken up by Bertrand Russell, who, with Alfred North Whitehead in their *Principia Mathematica*, attempted to describe all of mathematics in terms of the structure of logical systems. (Their project was ultimately and definitively refuted by Kurt Gödel, who developed a mathematical proof that demonstrated all logical systems were ultimately incomplete and couldn't account for all possible propositions.)

The idea that all language could be conceived in terms of logic was further explored by Russell's student Ludwig Wittgenstein. In his *Tractatus Logico-Philosophicus*, he put forward a number of propositions designed to demonstrate the way in which our description of the world we inhabit is limited by the language that we use to describe it. He ended with the provocative assertion that those things that could not be expressed in terms of language were things about which we should not speak at all.

This last claim was deeply influential on a school of Austrian philosophers who became known as the "logical positivists." This school of thought attempted to boil all language down to its most basic propositions, and rejected any claims that could not be tied directly to empirical data. As a result, it rejected all moral and religious claims as being without value; however, in the process, it also stripped language of much of its meaning and importance.

Wittgenstein later modified his approach to philosophy. In his *Philosophical Investigations*, he developed an approach to understanding language, not in terms of its logical structure per se, but rather in terms of "language-games," that is to say, rules-governed aspects of social life, the purpose of which is not simply to express ideas but to accomplish specific tasks. It is, in this sense, a pragmatic rather than an idealistic enterprise. What we express using language is not a pointer to some permanent external reality, but a means of expressing our experience in terms of the social setting in which we dwell.

This pragmatic approach to language is the aspect that has been most influential on contemporary philosophy. Wittgenstein's later philosophy, coupled with the approach of philosophers such as Alasdair MacIntyre and Richard Rorty and theologians such as William Placher and D. Z. Philips, have aided in the development of a theological approach that understands theological language as the expression of the language-game of a particular community, known as the church. This idea was influential on Yale School theologians such as Hans Frei and George Lindbeck, as well as students of theirs such as Stanley Hauerwas. While the various branches of this particular root spread out in many disparate directions, they are bound together in their interest in the way in which language forms the irreducible core of our experience in the world, including religious experience.

POST-MODERNISM

Postmodernism addresses many of the same concerns as the philosophy of language, although its pedigree comes from a different set of philosophical sources. Where linguistic philosophy is rooted in the empiricist and analytical philosophical tradition, postmodernism emerges from the continental tradition deriving initially from Kant and Hegel, the phenomenological approach of Husserl and Heidegger, the existentialism of Sartre, and the structuralism of Ferdinand de Saussure.

In a general sense (consensus being one of the difficult things to achieve within the movement), what is meant by postmodernism is skepticism with regard to any overarching metaphysical systems or explanations that seek to encapsulate human experience in its entirety. Postmodernism tends to reject "grand narratives" about the world and calls into question the presuppositions of philosophies that rely on them. Postmodernism is more about critique than construction, although some have argued that postmodernism does seek to construct a positive approach to philosophical inquiry, simply not one rooted in one singular story about the world.

The ranks of postmodern philosophers are legion, but two of its most prominent exemplars are Jacques Derrida and Michel Foucault. Both come from the French philosophical tradition, and though their approaches are often studied in conjunction, they are quite distinct.

Derrida's approach is often labeled as "deconstruction," which carries with it the idea that he is tearing down prior philosophical concepts and traditions. His approach tends to be playful and ironic. Often his work does not function as a direct critique but rather attempts to examine the inner contradictions within particular texts by showing how they rely on untenable binary alternatives that fall apart on close examination. Thus, for example, in *Of Grammatology* he calls into question the structuralist assumptions about the priority of speech to texts, arguing that texts have an integrity of their own independent of speech. Through this attempt to question what he terms "logocentrism," Derrida seeks to overcome the hierarchical relationships within philosophy.

In *Glas*, he takes a different approach. Juxtaposing Hegel's writing with that of the French playwright and provocateur Jean Genet, along with his own commentary, he calls into question the overarching metaphysical system represented by Hegel by forcing it into conversation with Genet's anarchic prose.

Through his writing Derrida attempts to demonstrate, in varying ways, that meaning is not fixed, nor is there a singular goal toward which philosophy in particular, or humankind in general, is going, except perhaps death. Rather, philosophy is about the

Postmodernism
Modernism

eternal deferral of meaning, which he demonstrates through a form of philosophical play.

Later in his life, Derrida developed a greater interest in religion, particularly as it intersects with political and ethical questions. He returned to a closer examination of his own Jewish background, in part under the influence of the philosopher Emmanuel Levinas. This influence can be seen, for example, in his use of Kierkegaard's thought in *The Gift of Death* as well as in his eulogy for Levinas, *Adieu, Emmanuel Levinas.*

While Derrida's thought has offered an influential critique of the metaphysical and epistemological dimensions of modernity, he has often been criticized for not giving sufficient attention to political questions. By contrast, Michel Foucault's philosophy has engaged such questions directly.

Central to Foucault's project is the analysis of power—who has it, how they get it, and how it is deployed. In works such as *The Birth of the Clinic* and *The Order of Things*, he engages in what he calls "archeology," tracing the historical process by which the categories through which we come to understand the world come into being, and demonstrating how they are rooted in and in the service of particular kinds of power relationships. Institutions create normative expectations about the nature of power, but those expectations are not necessary or natural; rather, they are themselves a reflection of how power is distributed within the systems that they represent. Hospitals, asylums, prisons, and other institutional forms create their own reality, which then goes unquestioned because it is expected.

For Foucault, there is not a distinction between what we know about the world and how we come to control or manipulate the world. In other words, power and knowledge are not separate things, but rather a singular entity, which he calls "power/knowledge." By questioning the basis of existing power relationships and the epistemological frameworks that undergird them, Foucault attempts to critique the moral and political presuppositions of contemporary society and the power relationships that support it. His work is thus overtly political and has been used in a variety of fields to critique the way in which categories of knowledge are used to support relationships of domination and subservience. For Foucault, these relationships of power/knowledge govern all areas of human thought, from hospitals and prisons to the way in which we understand sexuality. By breaking down our default understanding of what constitutes "normal" and recognizing the contingency of what we take for granted about the world, we can contemplate how it might be reconstructed.

As noted above, there are many divergent streams of postmodern thought, of which Derrida and Foucault represent only two. In many respects, postmodernism is less a philosophical movement than a generally skeptical disposition toward the possibility that the overarching questions that have motivated much of philosophy are finally susceptible to any definitive answer. Rather, all knowledge is local, and all understandings of the world are ultimately socially constructed. This pertains to questions of literature, art, religion, and every dimension of culture.

FEMINIST PHILOSOPHY

Feminist philosophy, as a particular approach to philosophical inquiry, is another relatively recent movement. Prior to the nineteenth century, there were few examples in Western thought of women writing and publishing on philosophical issues. Owing to the predominance of patriarchal social relationships and the marginalization of women in many intellectual areas, there were not ample opportunities for women to make contributions to the field.

One of the first major feminist philosophers was Mary Wollstonecraft. Writing primarily on ethical and political themes, she was one of the first and most articulate advocates for the full inclusion of women in political society in the late eighteenth and early nineteenth centuries. Her *Vindication of the Rights of Women* argued that women are entitled to education and equality with men within society.

Simone de Beauvior, whose work we considered earlier, was another significant contributor to the growth of feminism within philosophy, particularly in her *The Second Sex*. Drawing on existentialist themes, she argues that, by virtue of viewing women as mysteries rather than as fully fledged human beings, traditional philosophy has treated them as an "Other" (in the Hegelian sense), and thus denied them their own autonomy as free human beings. On the contrary, she argues, women possess no "essence" to which they are bound, but rather may choose their own way of being in the world. The radical freedom embodied by existentialism applies, she argues, just as much to women as to men. By reducing women to enigmas, society traps them within predetermined and traditional roles, viewing men as the standard model of human life and women as, in some sense, aberrant.

Within the last half century, feminism as a philosophical movement has developed and expanded considerably. Like postmodernism, it is a distinctly diverse movement, covering a range of fields and positions; there is no one singular feminist philosophy. For example, bell hooks writes feminist theory from the perspective of the African American experience, bringing questions of race and class to the center of the discussion, alongside gender.

Judith Butler argues that the category of gender itself is socially constructed, and that there is no *innate* quality to the gender roles that are imposed within society. Gender is "performed" through the adoption and internalization of particular categories of gender identity.

What all feminist philosophies share in common is their recognition of women's experience as a philosophically significant and morally important point of view, one that has historically been neglected by a philosophical tradition that has been done by, and oriented toward, men. In bringing women's experience to the

The thing that irks me the most is this shattered prison. I'm tired, tired of being enclosed here.

Emily Brontë, *Wuthering Heights*

center of the conversation, feminist theology calls into question what has been taken for granted in much prior philosophy.

Within theology, the feminist critique of patriarchy has been enormously significant, both in terms of the way in which it has enabled women to perceive themselves as equal members within the church, capable of and entitled to take on leadership, and in terms of how we speak about and conceive the nature of God. The idea that God is beyond gender implies that there is nothing innately privileged about referring to God as male, or in viewing the fact that Jesus Christ was male as representing a privileging of male experience within Christian life. On the contrary, feminist theologians have gone back to the biblical texts, reinterpreted them with a feminist lens, and discovered that the voices of women have been historically marginalized both within the Bible and the church.

FOR FURTHER READING

The set of texts that follow are intended to lead you deeper into your philosophical journey. What we have sought to do is provide the key primary texts that have informed the writing of this book, as well as several other primary works that have been central to the development of Christian theology. The goal is not to be comprehensive, but instructive. We hope that in moving from this volume into these texts, you will discover the many branching avenues of inquiry that form the history of philosophy.

The particular editions in this list were generally chosen on the basis of their availability and, in the case of translations, their relative fluency and easiness to read. The word "relative" is important here, since in some cases the texts would be difficult regardless of the translation. But wherever possible we have tried to find the translations that do the best job conveying their ideas in the clearest way. At the same time, where one text was seen as being the "standard" edition for a particular work, we have often chosen that one over others, in order to allow readers to be in conversation with the most authoritative rendition of the text.

For readers interested in further secondary literature on philosophy, there is, of course, a wealth of possibilities. Many introductory philosophy texts will touch on areas that are not directly germane to the development of Christian theology, but two texts in particular may be of use. The first is Fredrick Copleston's monumental *A History of Philosophy* (Image, 1993, reprint edition). Copleston was a Jesuit Priest and strong advocate for the Catholic belief in the consistency of faith with reason. This eleven volume history offers a comprehensive overview of philosophical thought from the ancient period to existentialism.

A briefer introduction can be found in Diogenes Allen's *Philosophy for Understanding Theology* (2nd ed., Westminster John Knox, 2007). The newest edition has been updated by Allen's former student Eric Springstead, who also collaborated with Allen on an important anthology of primary sources entitled *Primary Readings in Philosophy for Understanding Theology* (Westminster John Knox, 1997). These two volumes, read together, can helpfully build on the foundation laid in the current volume.

A final word on the organization of this list. Rather than a standard alphabetical bibliography, we have arranged this reading list by period and figure in chronological order. We have opted for a simplified citation style in order to make it as easy as possible for students to locate and read these texts.

ANCIENT PERIOD

G. S. Kirk, et al., *The Presocratic Philosophers: A Critical History With a Selection of Texts*. Cambridge University Press (1984).

Plato, *The Complete Dialogues*. Edith Hamilton, et al., eds. Princeton University Press (1961, 2005).

Plato, *The Republic*. Alan Bloom, trans. Basic Books (1991).

Aristotle, *The Basic Works of Aristotle*. Richard McKeon, ed. Random House (1941).

Aristotle, *The Nicomachean Ethics*. Oxford University Press (2009).

Aristotle, *Politics*. Oxford University Press (2009, reissue).

Marcus Tullius Cicero, *On Obligations (De Officiis)*. Oxford University Press (2008).

Epictetus, *Discourses, Fragments, Handbook*. Oxford University Press (2014).

John Dillon, *Neoplatonic Philosophy: Introductory Readings*. Hackett Publishing Company (2004).

Pseudo-Dionysius, *The Complete Works*. Paulist (1988).

MEDIEVAL PERIOD

Augustine, *On the Free Choice of the Will*. Hackett Publishing Company (1993).

John Scotus Eriugena, *Periphyseon on the Division of Nature*. Wipf & Stock (2011).

Anselm, *Monologion and Proslogion: With replies of Gaunilo and Anselm*. Hackett Publishing Company (1996).

Thomas Aquinas, *The Basic Writings of Thomas Aquinas* (2 vols.). Hackett Publishing Company (1997).

Thomas Aquinas, *Aquinas on Nature and Grace: Selections from the Summa Theologica*. Westminster John Knox (1954).

MODERN PERIOD

René Descartes, *Meditations on First Philosophy*. Hackett Publishing Company (1993).

Gottfried Wilhelm Leibniz, *Discourse on Metaphysics and Other Essays*. Hackett Publishing Company (1991).

Gottfried Wilhelm Leibniz, *Theodicy*. Open Court (1998).

Benedict de Spinoza, *Ethics*. Oxford University Press (2000).

Benedict de Spinoza, *Theologico-Political Treatise*. Cambridge University Press (2007).

John Locke, *An Essay Concerning Human Understanding*. Oxford University Press (1979).

John Locke, *A Letter Concerning Toleration*. Hackett Publishing Company (1983).

George Berkeley, *Three Dialogues Between Hylas and Philonous*. Hackett Publishing Company (1979).

David Hume, *An Enquiry Concerning Human Understanding: With Hume's Abstract of A Treatise of Human Nature and a Letter from a Gentleman to His Friend in Edinburgh*. Hackett Publishing Company (1993).

David Hume, *Dialogues Concerning Natural Religion*. Hackett Publishing Company (1998).

Mary Wollstonecraft, *A Vindication of the Rights of Women*. Norton (2009).

Immanuel Kant, *Prolegomena to Any Future Metaphysics*. 2nd ed. Hackett Publishing Company (2001).

Immanuel Kant, *Critique of Pure Reason*. Palgrave Macmillan (1997).

Immanuel Kant, *Grounding for the Metaphysics of Morals: With a Supposed Right to Lie Because of Philanthropic Concerns*. Hackett Publishing Company (1993).

Immanuel Kant, *Religion Within the Boundaries of Mere Reason: And Other Writings*. Cambridge University Press (1999).

NINETEENTH CENTURY

G. W. F. Hegel, *Phenomenology of Spirit*. Oxford University Press (1976).

G. W. F. Hegel, *Philosophy of Mind*. Oxford University Press (1971).

Ludwig Feuerbach, *The Essence of Christianity*. Prometheus Books (1989).

Karl Marx and Friedrich Engels, *The Marx-Engels Reader*. Norton (1978).

Søren Kierkegaard, *Stages on Life's Way*. Princeton University Press (1988).

Søren Kierkegaard, *Fear and Trembling/Repetition*. Princeton University Press (1983).

Friedrich Nietzsche, *On the Genealogy of Morals and Ecce Homo*. Vintage Books (1989).

Friedrich Nietzsche, *Beyond Good and Evil: Prelude to a Philosophy of the Future*. Vintage Books (1989).

TWENTIETH CENTURY

Bertrand Russell, *The Problems of Philosophy*. Von Schtupp (2013).

Alfred North Whitehead, *Process and Reality*. Free Press (1979).

Charles Hartshorne, *Anselm's Discovery: A Reexamination of the Ontological Proof of God's Existence*. Open Court (1991).

Edmund Husserl, *The Crisis of European Sciences and Transcendental Phenomenology: An Introduction to Phenomenological Philosophy*. Northwestern University Press (1970).

Martin Heidegger, *An Introduction to Metaphysics*. Yale University Press (1974).

Martin Heidegger, *Being and Time*. SUNY Press (2010).

Jean-Paul Sartre, *Existentialism and Human Emotions*. Citadel Books (2000).

Simone de Beauvoir, *The Ethics of Ambiguity*. Citadel Books (2000).

Simone de Beauvoir, *The Second Sex*. Vintage Books (2011).

Jacques Derrida, *Of Grammatology*. Johns Hopkins University Press (1998).

Jacques Derrida, *The Gift of Death*. University of Chicago Press (2007).

Michel Foucault, *The Birth of the Clinic*. Vintage Books (1994).

Michel Foucault, *The Order of Things*. Vintage Books (1994).

Judith Butler, *Gender Trouble: Feminism and the Subversion of Identity*. Routledge (2006).